PRAGMATICS
OF
JAPANESE
AS
NATIVE
AND
TARGET
LANGUAGE

PRAGMATICS
OF
JAPANESE
AS
NATIVE
AND
TARGET
LANGUAGE

edited by GABRIELE KASPER

SECOND LANGUAGE TEACHING & CURRICULUM CENTER
University of Hawai'i at Mānoa

Second Printing 1996

Funds for the publication of this technical report were provided in part by a grant to the University of Hawai‘i under the Language Resource Centers Program of the U. S. Department of Education.

ISBN 0–8248–1462–2

∞™ The paper used in this publication meets the minimum requirements of the American National Standard for Information Sciences—Permanence of Paper for Printed Library Materials.

ANSI Z39.48–1984

Distributed by
University of Hawai‘i Press
Order Department
2840 Kolowalu Street
Honolulu, HI 96822–1888

ABOUT THE NATIONAL FOREIGN LANGUAGE RESOURCE CENTER

THE SECOND LANGUAGE TEACHING AND CURRICULUM CENTER of the University of Hawai'i is a unit of the College of Languages, Linguistics, and Literature. Under a grant from the U.S. Department of Education, the Center has since 1990 served as a National Foreign Language Resource Center (NFLRC). The general direction of the Resource Center is set by a national advisory board. The Center conducts research, develops materials, and trains language professionals with the goal of improving foreign language instruction in the United States. The Center publishes research reports and teaching materials; it also sponsors a fellows program for senior scholars, an internship program, and a summer intensive teacher training institute. For additional information about Center programs, write:

Dr. Robert Bley-Vroman, Director
Second Language Teaching & Curriculum Center
Webster 203
2528 The Mall
University of Hawai'i
Honolulu, Hawai'i 96822

N F L R C ADVISORY BOARD

CONTENTS

PREFACE

THIS TECHNICAL REPORT includes three contributions to different areas of cross-cultural and interlanguage pragmatics:

1) A bibliography on the pragmatics of Japanese (Yoshinaga, Maeshiba, & Takahashi)

2) An investigation of the use of introspective data in research on interlanguage pragmatics (Robinson)

3) A study of the acquisition of the sentence-final particle *ne* by learners of Japanese as a second language (Sawyer).

Literature on Japanese pragmatics is not easily accessible through the usual bibliographical sources. In order achieve an overview of the current research situation on the pragmatics of Japanese, Naoko Yoshinaga, Naoko Maeshiba, and Satomi Takahashi compiled the bibliography included in this volume. In the context of our ongoing research on the teaching and learning of Japanese as a foreign language, the bibliography serves to identify literature which will provide useful descriptive frameworks, as well as point out research gaps which will have to be filled by future studies.

The bibliography includes theoretical, analytical, and empirical investigations of :

- the realization of different speech acts
- discourse organization
- conversational management
- honorifics
- gender-related differences in language use
- cultural and socio-psychological issues
- the acquisition of Japanese as L1 and L2
- the use of Japanese as L2
- the use of English as L2 by native speakers of Japanese
- the teaching of Japanese pragmatics.

We hope that the bibliography will be useful for a variety of research goals. At the same time, it clearly reflects our own research interests. A complete listing of titles has been attempted for speech act realization, discourse organization at the supra-sentential level, and conversational management. Since honorifics and gender-related language use are primarily sociolinguistic concerns, they have been covered more eclectically. The reason to include these areas is the real or virtual interaction of 'discernment politeness' (as expressed by honorifics and other linguistic means) with 'strategic politeness' (as implemented in speech act realization). Titles on Japanese culture and psychology, some of them explicitly contrastive to Western or specifically American counterparts, were included because such accounts provide an important explanatory framework for the understanding of Japanese sociopragmatics. Finally, studies of speech act realization in English by native speakers of Japanese were included because of the paucity of research on pragmatics in JSL/JFL, and because these studies provide both direct and indirect evidence for speech act realization in Japanese.

Mary Ann Robinson's study on the use of introspective reports in research on speech act realization continues our inquiry into methods of data collection in interlanguage pragmatics (cf. Kasper & Dahl 1991). Whereas a number of studies in the past used metapragmatic judgement tasks to probe into relatively stable states of pragmalinguistic or sociopragmatic knowledge, and multiple choice and reaction time were employed as behavioral measures to ascertain the on-line processing of pragmatic information (Takahashi 1990 for overview), subjects' verbal self-reports had not been used as a primary means of data collection in the published literature on learners' speech act production. The present study, which examines the production of refusals by Japanese speakers of English at two proficiency levels, combines a discourse completion task with concurrent think aloud reports and retrospective interviews. Both types of verbal report data shed light on a variety of planning decisions at the sociopragmatic and pragmalinguistic level, and the interaction of attended contextual cues and cultural schemata. Subjects also commented on the sources of their pragmatic knowledge and on task-specific aspects such as language of thoughts and processing difficulty. Robinson's study demonstrates convincingly that introspective methods can yield valuable information on states and processing of learners' pragmatic knowledge which is inaccessible through other data collection techniques. (After Robinson handed in her manuscript, it came to our attention that Cohen and Olshtain (1991) developed a similar design and arrived at similar results. Their study thus provides further encouraging evidence for the usability of verbal report data in the investigation of interlanguage speech act production.)

Mark Sawyer's study is one of the few to date which examine an aspect of learners' pragmatic knowledge developmentally. He reports on the acquisition of the sentence-final particle *ne* by adult second learners of Japanese with different L1 backgrounds. Since this particle is pervasive in spoken Japanese, relatively salient, and eminently useful, it is puzzling to observe that it develops late, compared to other particles, in most of these learners' interlanguage. Sawyer advances the hypothesis that the particle's late emergence may be due to its functioning at the affective rather than at the cognitive level, and the likelihood that the JSL classes in which the learners were enrolled emphasized the expression of referential meaning over relational meaning. Such a hypothesis had been proposed earlier with respect to foreign language learning in classroom settings (Kasper 1982). It is thus an issue worth exploring for SLA research whether adult L2 learners assign different priorities to fundamental communicative functions (referential vs.

relational), and if such priorities vary with learning context (SL, FL, mixed). As for the teaching of JSL/JFL, it would seem important to examine the availability in teacher talk of affectively oriented linguistic items such as the particle *ne*, and the opportunity afforded to students to use such items productively in classroom tasks.

REFERENCES

Cohen, A.D., & Olshtain, E. (1991). *The production of speech acts by nonnatives*. Paper presented at the conference 'Theory construction and research methodology in second language acquisition', Lansing, MI, October 1991.

Kasper, G. (1982). Teaching-induced errors in interlanguage discourse. *Studies in Second Language Acquisition, 4*, 99–113.

Kasper, G., & Dahl, M. (1991). Research methods in interlanguage pragmatics. *Studies in Second Language Acquisition, 13*, 215–247. Also in *Technical Report #1*, Honolulu, Hawai'i: University of Hawai'i, Second Language Teaching & Curriculum Center.

Takahashi, S. (1990). Exploring comprehension processes of nonliteral utterances and some implications for automaticity. *University of Hawai'i Working Papers in English as a Second Language, 9*(2), 67–97.

Naoko Yoshinaga, Naoko Maeshiba, & Satomi Takahashi

BIBLIOGRAPHY
ON
JAPANESE
PRAGMATICS

Alpatov, V. M., & Kryuchkova, T. B. (1980). O muzhskom i zhenskom variantakh yaponskogo yazyka [Male and female variants of the Japanese language]. *Voprosy Yazykoznaniya* [Questions in Language Studies], *29*, 58–68.

Aoki, H. (1986). Evidentials in Japanese. In W. L. Chafe & J. Nichols (Eds.), *Evidentiality: The linguistic coding of epistemology* (pp. 223–238). Norwood, NJ: Ablex.

Aoki, H., & Okamoto, S. (1988). *Rules for conversational rituals in Japanese*. Tokyo: Taishukan.

Arima, M. (1989). Japanese culture versus schizophrenic interpretation. *Text, 9*, 351–365.

Arndt, H., & Janney, R. W. (in press). Universality and relativity in cross-cultural politeness research: A historical perspective. *Multilingua*.

Ashworth, D. (1975). Bunka ni kakawaru nihongo no daimeishi [Japanese pronouns in relation to culture]. In M. Nobayashi (Ed.), *Shinnihongo kooza, Volume 10* [New Japanese, Volume 10] (pp. 223–242). Tokyo: Sekibunsha.

Barnlund, D. (1975). Communicative styles in two cultures: Japan and the United States. In A. Kendon, R. Harris, & M. R. Key (Eds.), *Organization of behavior in face–to–face interaction* (pp.427–ß456). Hague: Mouton.

Barnlund, D. (1975). *Public and private self in Japan and the United States: Communicative styles of two cultures*. Tokyo: Saimul.

Beebe, L. M., & Takahashi, T. (1989). Do you have a bag?: Social status and patterned variation in second language acquisition. In S. Gass, C. Madden, D. Preston, & L. Selinker (Eds.), *Variation in second language acquisition: Discourse and pragmatics* (pp. 103–125). Clevedon: Multilingual Matters.

Beebe, L. M., & Takahashi, T. (1989). Sociolinguistic variation in face-threatening speech acts: Chastisement and disagreement. In M. Eisenstein (Ed.), *The dynamic interlanguage* (pp. 199–218). New York: Plenum.

Yoshinaga, Y., Maeshiba, M.. & Takahashi, S. (1991). Pragmatics on Japanese bibliography. In G. Kasper (Ed.), *Pragmatics of Japanese as native and target language* (Technical Report #3) (pp. 1–26). Honolulu, Hawai'i: University of Hawai'i, Second Language Teaching & Curriculum Center.

Beebe, L. M., Takahashi, T., & Uliss-Weltz, R. (1990). Pragmatic transfer in ESL refusals. In R. C. Scarcella, E. S. Andersen, & S. D. Krashen (Eds.), *Developing communicative competence in a second language* (pp. 55–73). New York: Newbury House.

Benedict, R. (1947). *The chrysanthemum and the sword: Patterns of Japanese culture*. London: Secker & Warburg.

Chafe, W. L. (1986). Evidentiality in English conversation and academic writing. In W. L. Chafe & J. Nichols (Eds.), *Evidentiality: The linguistic coding of epistemology* (pp. 261–272). Norwood, NJ: Ablex.

Chafe, W. L., & Nichols, J. (Eds.). (1986). *Evidentiality: The linguistic coding of epistemology*. Norwood, NJ: Ablex.

Clancy, P. M. (1980). Referential choice in English and Japanese narrative discourse. In W. L. Chafe (Ed.), *The pear stories: Cognitive, cultural, and linguistic aspects of narrative production* (pp. 124–199). Norwood, NJ: Ablex.

Clancy, P. M. (1982). Written and spoken style in Japanese narratives. In D. Tannen (Ed.), *Spoken and written language: Exploring orality and literacy* (pp. 55–76). Norwood, NJ: Ablex.

Clancy, P. M. (1985). The acquisition of Japanese. In D. I. Slobin (Ed.), *The crosslinguistic study of language acquisition* (pp. 373–524). Hillsdale, NJ: Erlbaum.

Clancy, P. M. (1986). The acquisition of communicative style in Japanese. In B. Schieffelin & E. Ochs (Eds.), *Language socialization across cultures* (pp. 213–249). Cambridge: Cambridge University Press.

Condon, J. C. & Saito, M. (Eds.) (1974). *Intercultural encounters with Japan: Communication — contact and conflict*. Tokyo: Saimul.

Cook, H. M. (1985). Frequency of nominal markers in the speech of a Japanese child and his caretakers: A case study. *Descriptive and Applied Linguistics, 18*, 13–24.

Cook, H. M. (1987). *Group and individual evidentials: Sentence-final no and bare verbs in Japanese*. Paper presented at the Linguistics Society of American Meeting, San Francisco.

Cook, H. M. (1987). Social meanings of the Japanese sentence-final particle *no*. *IPrA Papers in Pragmatics, 1*, 123–148.

Cook, H. M. (1988). *The Japanese -masu suffix as an indexical of affective distance*. Paper presented at the Honorifics Conference, Portland, OR.

Cook, H. M. (1988). *Sentential particles in Japanese conversation: A study of indexicality*. Unpublished doctoral dissertation, University of Southern California, Los Angeles.

Cook, H. M. (1990). An indexical account of the Japanese sentence-final particle *no*. *Discourse Processes, 13*, 401–439.

Cook, H. M. (1990). *Meanings of non-referential indexes: A case study of the Japanese sentence-final particle ne*. Manuscript submitted for publication.

Cook, H. M. (1990). The role of the Japanese sentence-final particle *no* in the socialization of children. *Multilingua, 9*, 377–395.

Coulmas, F. (1980). Zur Personaldeixis im Japanischen [On person deixis in Japanese]. *Papiere zur Linguistik, 2*, 3–19.

Coulmas, F. (1982). Some remarks on Japanese deictics. In J. Weissenborn & W. Klein (Eds.), *Here and there* (pp. 209–221). Amsterdam: John Benjamins.

Coulmas, F. (1987). *Keigo*—Höflichkeit und soziale Bedeutung im Japanischen [*Keigo*—politeness and social meaning in Japanese]. *Linguistische Berichte, 107*, 44–62.

Coulmas, F. (1987). Why speak English? In K. Knapp, W. Enninger, & A Knapp-Potthoff (Eds.), *Analyzing intercultural communication* (pp. 95–107). Berlin: Mouton de Gruyter.

Daikuhara, M. (1986). A study of compliments from a cross-cultural perspective: Japanese vs. American English. *Penn Working Papers in Educational Linguistics, 2* (2), 103–134.

Dasher, R. (1982). The semantic development of honorific expressions in Japanese. *Papers in Linguistics, 15*, 217–228.

DeVos, G. (1985). Dimensions of the self in Japanese culture. In A. Marsella, D. DeVos, & F. Hsu (Eds.), *Culture and self: Asian and Western perspectives* (pp. 141–184). New York: Tavistock.

Doi, T. (1956). Japanese language as an expression of Japanese psychology. *Western Speech*, *20*, 90–96.

Doi, T. (1971). *Amae no koozoo*. Tokyo: Kobunsha. English translation: *The anatomy of dependence*. Tokyo: Kodansha International, 1973.

Doi, T. (1974). Some psychological themes in Japanese human relationships. In J. C. Condon & M. Saito (Eds.), *Intercultural encounters with Japan: Communication — contact and conflict* (pp.17–26). Tokyo: Saimul.

Doi, T. (1985). *Omote to ura*. Tokyo: Kobundo. English translation: *The anatomy of self: The individual versus society*. Tokyo: Kodansha International, 1986.

Fischer, J. L. (1970). Linguistic socialization: Japan and the United States. In R. Hill & R. König (Eds.), *Families in East and West* (pp. 107–119). Paris: Mouton.

Fukushima, S. (1990). Offers and requests: Performance by Japanese learners of English. *World Englishes*, *9*, 317–325.

Fukushima, S., & Iwata, Y. (1987). Politeness strategies in requesting and offering. *JACET Bulletin*, *18*, 31–48.

Goldstein, B. Z., & Tamura, K. (1975). *Japan and America: A comparative study in language and culture*. Tokyo: Charles E. Tuttle Co.

Hashiuchi, T. (1988). Kaiwa no shikumi o saguru [A study of conversational structure]. *Nihongogaku* [Japanese Linguistics], *7*, 43–51.

Hata, H. (1982). Komyunikeeshon no tame no nihongo kyoiku [Teaching Japanese for communication]. *Gengo* [Language], *December*, 56–71.

Hata, H. (1983). Bamen to kotoba [Context and language]. *Kokugo Gaku* [Study of Japanese Language], *133*, 55–68.

Hata, H. (1986). Kaigi no puragumatikkusu [The pragmatics of conferences]. *Gengo Seikatsu* [Language Life], *415*, 38–45.

Hata, H. (1988). Gaikokujin no tame no nihongo kaiwa sutoratejii to sono kyoiku [The Teaching of Japanese conversation strategies]. *Nihongogaku* [Japanese Linguistics], *7*, 101–117.

Hayashi, R. (1987). *A study of floor management of English and Japanese conversation*. Unpublished doctoral dissertation, University of Illinois at Urbana-Champaign, Urbana, IL.

Hayashi, R. (1988). Simultaneous talk from the perspective of floor management of English and Japanese speakers. *World Englishes*, *7*, 269–288.

Hayashi, R. (1990). Rhythmicity, sequence and synchrony as floor management in English and Japanese face-to-face conversation. *Language Sciences*, *12*, 155–195.

Hayashi, R. (1991). Floor structure of English and Japanese. *Journal of Pragmatics*, *16*, 1–30.

Hayashi, S. (1979). Taijin kankei to kotoba [Human relations and language]. *Gengo Seikatsu* [Language Life], *295*, 18–29.

Hayashi, S. (1983). Nihongo no bun no katachi to shisei [Japanese sentence structure and sentence types]. In Kokuritsu Kokugo Kenkyusho [National Language Research Institute] (Ed.), *Danwa no kenkyu to kyoiku I* [The study of discourse in teaching Japanese I] (pp. 43–62). Tokyo: Okurasho Insatsukyoku.

Hayashi, S. (1989). Nihongo kyoiku ni okeru bunka no mondai [Issues of culture in teaching Japanese]. *Nihongo gaku* [Japanese Linguistics], *8*, 14–20.

Higa, M. (1972). The use of the imperative mood in post–war Japan. In W. P. Lebra (Ed.), *Transcultural research in mental health* (pp. 49–56). Honolulu: University of Hawai'i Press.

Hijirida, K. & Sohn, H. (1986). Cross–cultural patterns of honorifics and sociolinguistic sensitivity to honorific variables: Evidence from English, Japanese, and Korean. *Papers in Linguistics*, *19*, 365–401.

Hill, B., Ide, S., Ikuta, S., Kawasaki, A., & Ogino, T. (1986). Universals of linguistic politeness: Quantitative evidence from Japanese and American English. *Journal of Pragmatics*, *10*, 347–371.

Hinata, N. (1989). Nihonjin to aisatsu suru toki no muzukashisa: Burajirujin no baai [Difficulty in greetings in Japanese: Case of Brazilians]. *Nihongogaku* [Japanese Linguistics], 8, 72–77.

Hinds, J. (1976). A taxonomy of Japanese discourse types. *Linguistics*, 184, 45–53.

Hinds, J. (1976). *Aspects of Japanese discourse structure*. Tokyo: Kaitakusha.

Hinds, J. (1977). Conversational structures. In J. Hinds (Ed.), *Proceedings of the 2nd HATJ-UH Conference on Japanese Language and Linguistics* (pp. 52–81). Honolulu.

Hinds, J. (1982). Japanese conversational structures. *Lingua*, 57, 301–326.

Hinds, J. (1983). Intrusion in Japanese conversation. *Papers in Linguistics*, 16, 1–33. Also in S. Miyagawa & C. Kitagawa (Eds.), (1984), *Studies in Japanese language use* (pp. 1–33). Carbondale, IL: Linguistic Research, Inc.

Holden, N. (1983). The Japanese language: A partial view from the inside. *Multilingua*, 2, 157–166.

Honna, N. & Hoffer, B. (1989). *An English dictionary of Japanese ways of thinking*. Tokyo: Yuhikaku.

Hori, M. (1986). A sociolinguistic analysis of the Japanese honorifics. *Journal of Pragmatics*, 10, 373–386.

Horodeck, R. (1981). Excuses and apologies: Discovering how they work with the game. *Journal of the Association of Teachers of Japanese*, 16, 119–139.

Hoshino, A. (1989). Mainasu keigo to shite no keihigo, bago, warukuchi [Keihigo and bago (cursing and swearing) as minus honorific expressions in Japanese language teaching]. *Nihongo Kyoiku* [Journal of Japanese Language Teaching], 69, 110–120.

Ide, S. (1973). Nichibei taisho teinei hyogenron—shakaigengogakuteki kosatsu [Contrastive theory of Japanese and English polite expressions—sociolinguistic considerations]. *Eigo Kyoiku* [The English Teacher's Magazine], 22 (10), 19–22.

Ide, S. (1982). Japanese sociolinguistics: Politeness and women's language. *Lingua*, *57*, 357–385.

Ide, S. (1989). Formal forms and discernment: Two neglected aspects of linguistic politeness. *Multilingua*, *8*, 223–248.

Ide, S., Hori, M., Kawasaki, A., Ikuta, S., & Haga, H. (1986). Sex differences and politeness in Japanese. *International Journal of the Sociology of Language*, *58*, 25–36.

Ikegami, Y. (1983). Tekusuto to tekusuto no koozoo [Text and its structure]. In Kokuritsu Kokugo Kenkyusho [National Language Research Institute] (Ed.), *Danwa no kenkyu to kyoiku I* [The study of discourse in teaching Japanese I] (pp. 7–42). Tokyo: Okurasho Insatsukyoku.

Ikegami, Y. (1989). Discourse analysis in Japan: Introduction. *Text*, *9*, 263–273.

Ikuta, S. (1988). Strategies of requesting in Japanese conversational discourse. *Dissertation Abstracts International*, *49*, 245–A.

Inoue, K. (1983). Some discourse principles and lengthy sentences in Japanese. *Papers in Linguistics*, *16*, 57–87. Also in S. Miyagawa & C. Kitagawa (Eds.), (1984), *Studies in Japanese language use* (pp. 57–87). Carbondale, IL: Linguistic Research, Inc.

Ishikawa, A., Nagata, T., Miyai, M., Nagao, A., & Iizuka, H. (1981). Address terms in modern Japanese: A sociolinguistic analysis. *Sophia Linguistica*, *8/9*, 129–141.

Ito, Y. (1989). Strategies of disagreement: A comparison of Japanese and American usage. *Sophia Linguistica*, *27*, 193–202.

Jinnouchi, M. (1988). Gengohenshu to supiichi sutairu [Language variety and speech style]. *Nihongogaku* [Japanese Linguistics], *7*, 77–88.

Kageyama, T. & Tamori, I. (1976). Japanese whimperatives. *Papers in Japanese Linguistics*, *4*, 13–53.

Kamio, A. (1979). On the notion of speaker's territory of information: A functional analysis of certain sentence-final forms in Japanese. In G. Bedell, E. Kobayashi, & M. Muraki (Eds.), *Explorations in linguistics: Papers in honor of Kazuko Inoue* (pp. 213–231). Tokyo: Kenkyusha.

Kawaguchi, G. (1987). Nihongo shokyu kyokasho ni okeru keigo no atsukaware kata [How honorifics are handled in beginning level textbooks]. *Nihongo Kyoiku* [Journal of Japanese Language Teaching], *61*, 126–139.

Kinoshita, K. (1988). Language habits of the Japanese. *English Today*, *4*, 19–25. Also in *The Bulletin of the Association for Business Communication*, *51*, (1988), 35–40.

Kishitani, S. (1969). Der Japanische Honorativ und seine Verwendung in der Sprache der Gegenwart [The Japanese honorative and its use in the contemporary language]. In B. Lewin (Ed.), *Beiträge zum interpersonalen Bezug im Japanischen* [Contributions to interpersonal reference in Japanese] (pp. 1–17). Wiesbaden: Otto Harrassowitz.

Kishitani, S. (1985). Die japanische Auffassung der personalen Beziehung gezeigt an Beispielen der Höflichkeitsformen [The Japanese notion of personal relationships, illustrated by the honorifics]. In S. Kishitani (Ed.), *Die Person in der Satzaussage* [The person in sentence predication] (pp. 238–267). Wiesbaden: Otto Harrassowitz.

Kitagawa, C. (1980). Saying "yes" in Japanese. *Journal of Pragmatics*, *4*, 105–120.

Kitao, K. (1988). Differences between politeness strategies used in requests by Americans and Japanese. *Doshisha Studies in English*, *44–45*, 326–343.

Kitao, K., & Kitao, S. K. (1988). Poraitonesu [Politeness]. *Nihongogaku* [Japanese Linguistics], *7*, 52–63.

Klopf, D. W. (1991). Japanese communication practices: Recent comparative research. *Communication Quarterly*, *39*, 130–143.

Koide, F. (1974). Some observations on the Japanese language. In J. C. Condon & M. Saito (Eds.), *Intercultural encounters with Japan* (pp. 173–179). Tokyo: Saimul Press.

Koizumi, T. (1990). *Gengai no gengogaku: Nihongo goyooron* [Implicational linguistics: Japanese pragmatics]. Tokyo: Sanseidoo.

Kumatoridani, T. (1988). Hatsuwa kooi riron to danwa koodoo kara mita nihongo no wabi to kansha [Japanese apologies and gratitude from the perspectives of speech act theory and discourse behavior]. *Hiroshima Daigaku Kyoikugakubu Kiyou Dai ni bu* [Hiroshima University Department of Education Bulletin II], *37*, 223–234.

Kumatoridani, T. (1989). Terebi komaasharu ni okeru settoku koodoo [Persuasion behavior in television commercials]. *Nihongo Kyoiku* [Journal of Japanese Language Teaching], *67*, 72–86.

Kuroda, S. Y. (1973). Where epistemology, style, and grammar meet: A case study from Japanese. In S. R. Anderson & P. Kiparsky (Eds.), *A festschrift for Morris Halle* (pp. 377–391). New York: Holt, Rinehart, and Winston.

Kurokawa, S. (1972). Japanese terms of address: Some usages of the first and second person pronouns. *Papers in Japanese Linguistics, 1*, 228–238.

Lanham, B. B. (1986). Ethics and moral precepts taught in schools of Japan and the United States. In T. S. Lebra & W. P. Lebra (Eds.), *Japanese culture and behavior: Selected readings* (revised edition) (pp. 280–296). Honolulu: University of Hawai'i Press.

Lebra, T. S. (1974). Reciprocity and the asymmetric principle: An analytic reappraisal of the Japanese concept of On. In T. S. Lebra & W. P. Lebra (Eds.), *Japanese culture and behavior: Selected readings* (pp. 192–207). Honolulu: University of Hawai'i Press.

Lebra, T. S. (1976). *Japanese patterns of behavior*. Honolulu: University of Hawai'i Press.

Lebra, T. S. (1987). The cultural significance of silence in Japanese communication. *Journal of Cross-cultural and Interlanguage Communication, 6–4*, 343–357.

Lebra, T. S., & Lebra, W. P. (Eds.). (1974). *Japanese culture and behavior: Selected readings*. Honolulu: University of Hawai'i Press.

Lebra, T. S., & Lebra, W. P. (Eds.). (1986). *Japanese culture and behavior: Selected readings* (revised edition). Honolulu: University of Hawai'i Press.

Lewin, B. (1967). The understanding of Japanese honorifics: A historical approach. In J. K. Yamagiwa (Ed.), *Papers of the CIC Far Eastern Language Institute* (pp. 107–125). Ann Arbor: University of Michigan Press.

Lewin, B. (1969). *Beiträge zum interpersonalen Bezug im Japanischen* [Contributions to interpersonal reference in Japanese]. Wiesbaden: Otto Harrassowitz.

Lewin, B. (1969). Honorative Sprachformen des Japanischen im Zeitalter der Demokratisierung [Japanese honorifics in the age of democratization]. In B. Lewin (Ed.), *Beiträge zum interpersonalen Bezug im Japanischen* [Contributions to interpersonal reference in Japanese] (pp. 167–184). Wiesbaden: Otto Harrassowitz.

LoCastro, V. (1987). Aizuchi: A Japanese conversational routine. In L. E. Smith (Ed.), *Discourse across cultures* (pp. 101–113). New York: Prentice Hall.

Loveday, L. (1981). Pitch, politeness, and sexual role: An exploratory investigation into the pitch correlates of English and Japanese politeness formulae. *Language and Speech, 24,* 71–89.

Loveday, L. (1982). Communicative interference: A framework for contrastively analysing L2 communicative competence exemplified with the linguistic behavior of Japanese performing in English. *International Review of Applied Linguistics in Language Teaching, 20,* 1–16.

Loveday, L. (1982). Japanese donatory forms: Their implications for linguistic theory. *Studia Linguistica, 36,* 39–63.

Loveday, L. (1983). Rhetoric patterns in conflict: The sociocultural relativity of discourse-organizing processes. *Journal of Pragmatics, 7,* 169–190.

Loveday, L. (1985). At cross-purposes: Semiotic schism in Japanese-Western interaction. In R. J. Brunt & W. Enninger (Eds.), *Interdisciplinary perspectives at cross-cultural communication* (pp. 31–63). Aachen: Rader.

Loveday, L. (1986). *Explorations in Japanese sociolinguistics*. Amsterdam: John Benjamins.

Loveday, L. (1986). Japanese sociolinguistics: An introductory survey. *Journal of Pragmatics, 10*, 287–326.

Loveday, L., & Chiba, S. (1985). Partaking with the divine and symbolizing the societal: The semiotics of Japanese food and drink. *Semiotica, 56*, 115–131.

Makino, S. (1970). Two proposals about Japanese polite expressions. In J. Sadock & A. Vanek (Eds.), *Studies presented to R. B. Lees by his students* (pp. 163–187). Edmonton, Alberta: Linguistic Research Inc.

Makino, S. (1983). Speaker/listener orientation and formality marking in Japanese. *Gengo Kenkyu* [Study of Language], *84*, 126–145.

Makino, S. (1987). How relevant is a functional notion of communicative orientation to *wa* and *ga?* In J. Hinds, S. K. Maynard, & S. Iwasaki (Eds.), *Perspectives in topicalization: Case of Japanese wa* (pp. 293–306). Amsterdam: John Benjamins.

Markus, H. R., & Kitayama, S. (1991). Culture and the self: Implications for cognition, emotion, and motivation. *Psychological Review, 98*, 224–253.

Martin, S. E. (1964). Speech levels in Japan and Korea. In D. Hymes (Ed.), *Language in culture and society* (pp. 407–415). New York: Harper and Row.

Mase, Y., Okano, H., & Ito, S. (1989). Gaikokujin no gengo koodoo ni taisuru nihonjin no ishiki [Japanese reactions toward foreigners' linguistic behavior]. *Nihongo Kyoiku* [Journal of Japanese Language Teaching], *67*, 25–27.

Matsumoto, Y. (1979). Linguistic behavior of Americans in Japan: A case study of American businessmen in Tokyo. *Working Papers on Bilingualism in Japan.*

Matsumoto, Y. (1981). Bilingualism among American businessmen in Tokyo. In F. C. C. Peng & M. Hori (Eds.), *Language as social behavior: Sociolinguistics series no. 3*. Hiroshima: Bunka Hyooron.

Matsumoto, Y. (1985). A sort of speech act qualification in Japanese: *Chotto*. *Journal of Asian Culture*, 9, 143–159.

Matsumoto, Y. (1986). Review of *Japanese women's language*. *Studies in Second Language Acquisition*, 8, 238–241.

Matsumoto, Y. (1988). Re-examination of the universality of face: Politeness phenomena in Japanese. *Journal of Pragmatics*, 12, 403–426.

Matsumoto, Y. (1988). Semantics and pragmatics of noun-modifying constructions in Japanese. *Proceedings of the Fourteenth Annual Meeting of the Berkeley Linguistic Society*, 166–175.

Matsumoto, Y. (1989). Japanese style noun modification in English. *Proceedings of the Fifteenth Annual Meeting of the Berkeley Linguistics Society*, 226–237.

Matsumoto, Y. (1989). Politeness and conversational universals— observations from Japanese. *Multilingua*, 8, 207–222.

Matsumoto, Y. (1990). *Honorifics in subordinate clauses*. Paper presented at the Annual Meeting of the Mid-Atlantic Region of the Association for Asian Studies, NJ.

Matsumoto, Y. (1990). *Speech act qualification revisited*. Paper presented at the International Pragmatics Conference, Barcelona, Spain.

Matsumoto, Y. (1991). *Cultural relativity in theories of politeness: Arguments from Japanese (or, being nice without Grice)*. Paper presented at the conference "New Departures in Contrastive Linguistics," Innsbruck, Austria.

Matsumoto, Y. (1991). Role of pragmatics in Japanese relative clauses. *Lingua*, 82, 111–129.

Matsumoto, Y. (in press). Acquisition of Japanese by American businessmen in Tokyo: How much and why. In C. Blackshire-Belay (Ed.), *Handbook of second language acquisition*. Tübingen: Narr.

Matsumoto, Y. (in press). Review of *MacArthur's Japanese constitution: A linguistic and cultural study of its making. Language*.

Maynard, S. K. (1980). *Discourse functions of the Japanese theme marker - w a*. Unpublished doctoral dissertation, Northwestern University, Evanston, IL.

Maynard, S. K. (1984). Functions of *to* and *koto-o* in speech and thought representation in Japanese written discourse. *Lingua, 64*, 1–24.

Maynard, S. K. (1989). Functions of the discourse marker *dakara* in Japanese conversation. *Text, 9*, 389–414.

Maynard, S. K. (1989). *Japanese conversation*. Norwood, NJ: Ablex.

Maynard, S. K. (1991). Pragmatics of discourse modality: A case of *da* and *desu/masu* forms in Japanese. *Journal of Pragmatics, 15*, 551–582.

McCrath, E. (1977). Acculturation in the classroom. In J. Hinds (Ed.), *Proceedings of the 2nd HATJ-UH Conference on Japanese Language and Linguistics* (pp. 122–128). Honolulu.

McGloin, N. H. (1976/77). The speaker's attitude and the conditionals *to, tara,* and *ba. Papers in Japanese Linguistics, 5*, 181–191.

McGloin, N. H. (1980). Some observations concerning *no desu* expressions. *Journal of the Association of Teachers of Japanese, 15*, 117–149.

McGloin, N. H. (1983). Some politeness strategies in Japanese. *Papers in Linguistics, 16*, 127–145. Also in S. Miyagawa & C. Kitagawa (Eds.), (1984), *Studies in Japanese language use* (pp. 127–145). Carbondale, IL: Linguistic Research, Inc.

McGloin, N. H. (1986). Feminine *wa* and *no*: Why do women use them? *Journal of the Association of Teachers of Japanese, 20*, 7–27.

Mey, J. L. (Ed.). (1986). Japanese sociolinguistics [Special issue]. *Journal of Pragmatics, 10*.

Miller, A. R. (1971). Levels of speech (keigo) and the Japanese linguistic response to modernization. In D. H. Shively (Ed.), *Tradition and modernization in Japanese culture* (pp. 601–665). Princeton: Princeton University Press.

Minami, F. (1983). Danwa no tani [Units of discourse]. In Kokuritsu Kokugo Kenkyusho [National Language Research Institute] (Ed.), *Danwa no kenkyu to kyoiku I* [The study of discourse in teaching Japanese I] (pp. 91–112). Tokyo: Okurasho Insatsukyoku.

Miyagawa, S. &. Kitagawa, C. (Eds.) (1984). *Studies in Japanese language use*. Carbondale, IL: Linguistic Research, Inc.

Miyagawa, S. (1982). Requesting in Japanese. *Journal of the Association of Teachers of Japanese, 17,* 123–142.

Miyagawa, S. (1983). Pragmatics of causation in Japanese. *Papers in Linguistics, 16,* 147–184. Also in S. Miyagawa & C. Kitagawa (Eds.), (1984), *Studies in Japanese language use* (pp. 147–184). Carbondale, IL: Linguistic Research, Inc.

Miyaji, Y. (1957). Keigo no konran [Confusion in honorific expressions]. *Gengo Seikatsu* [Language Life], *70,* (7), 26–34.

Miyamoto, M. (1989). Watashi to nihongo, nihon bunka: Ibunka sesshoku toshite no nihongo gakushu [My experience with Japanese language and culture: Japanese language learning as cross-cultural encounter]. *Nihongogaku* [Japanese Linguistics], 8 (12), 66–71.

Mizutani, N. (1982). The listener's response in Japanese conversation. *Sociolinguistic Newsletter, 13* (1), 33–38.

Mizutani, N. (1983). Aizuchi to ootoo [Backchanneling and responding]. In O. Mizutani (Ed.), *Hanashi kotoba no hyogen* [Expressions in spoken language] (pp. 37–44). Tokyo: Chikuma Shoboo.

Mizutani, N. (1984). Nihongo kyoiku to hanashikotoba no jittai: Aizuchi no bunseki [Teaching Japanese and the reality of spoken language: An analysis of backchanneling]. In *Kindaiichi Haruhiko hakase koki kinen ronbunshuu* [In honor of Dr. Haruhiko Kindaiichi on his 70th birthday] (pp. 261–279). Tokyo: Sanseidoo.

Mizutani, N. (1989). Taiguu hyogen shido no hoho [Teaching politeness in Japanese]. *Nihongo Kyoiku* [Journal of Japanese Language Teaching], 69, 24–35.

Mizutani, O. (1979). Hanashi kotoba to nihonjin: *Nihongo no seitai*. Tokyo: Sotakusha. English translation: Japanese: *The spoken language in Japanese life*. Tokyo: Japan Times, 1981.

Mizutani, O., & Mizutani, N. (1987). *How to be polite in Japanese*. Tokyo: The Japan Times.

Moeran, B. (1988). Japanese language and society: An anthropological approach. *Journal of Pragmatics, 12*, 427–443.

Monane, T. A., & Rogers, L. W. (1977). Cognitive features of Japanese language and culture and their implications for language teaching. In J. Hinds (Ed.), *Proceedings of the 2nd HATJ-UH Conference on Japanese Language and Linguistics* (pp. 129–137). Honolulu.

Morita, K. (1974). Language and thought in Japan: A theory of the influence of Japanese language and cognition. In J. C. Condon & M. Saito (Eds.), *Intercultural encounters with Japan* (pp. 196–198). Tokyo: Saimul Press.

Morita, Y. (1989). Renbun kei [Patterns of coordination]. In Kokuritsu Kokugo Kenkyusho [National Language Research Institute] (Ed.), *Danwa no kenkyu to kyoiku II* [The study of discourse in teaching Japanese II] (pp. 113–202). Tokyo: Okurasho Insatsukyoku.

Moriya, T. (1988). *Mada, moo* vs. *already, yet, still, anymore*: Comparison of time adverbs in Japanese and English. *Sophia Linguistica, 26*, 101–111.

Morosawa, A. (1988). Requesting in Japanese: A psycholinguistic investigation. *Sophia Linguistica, 16*, 129–137.

Morosawa, A. (1990). Intimacy and urgency in request forms of Japanese: A psycholinguistic study. *Sophia Linguistica, 28*, 129–143.

Nagano, K. (1983). Danwa ni okeru jojutsu no koozoo [Narrative structure in discourse]. In Kokuritsu Kokugo Kenkyusho [National Language Research Institute] (Ed.), *Danwa no kenkyu to kyoiku I* [The study of discourse in teaching Japanese I] (pp. 63–90). Tokyo: Okurasho Insatsukyoku.

Nakada, T. (1989). Hatsuwa kooi to shite no chinsha to kansha [Apology and thanks in Japanese and English]. *Nihongo Kyoiku* [Journal of Japanese Language Teaching], *68*, 191–203.

Nakamichi, M., Hata, I., Saegusa, R., & Baba, R. (1989). Go no "Taisha teki tokucho": Taisha teki taido no hyogen no gengokan hikaku [Interpersonal attitude and its indication in Japanese, English, German, and Portuguese]. *Nihongo Kyoiku* [Journal of Japanese Language Teaching], *69*, 64–76.

Nakane, C. (1970). *Japanese society.* London: Weidenfeld & Nicolson.

Nakane, C. (1972). *Human relations in Japan: Summary translation of "Tateshakai no ningen kankei"* [Personal relations in a vertical society]. Tokyo: Ministry of Foreign Affairs.

Nakane, C. (1974). The social system reflected in interpersonal communication. In J. C. Condon & M. Saito (Eds.), *Intercultural encounters with Japan* (pp. 124–198). Tokyo: Saimul Press.

Naotsuka, R., & Sakamoto, N. (1981). *Mutual understanding of different cultures.* Tokyo: Taishukan.

Neustupny, J. V. (1978). The variability of Japanese honorifics. *Proceedings of the symposium on Japanese sociolinguistics* (pp. 125–150). San Antonio: Trinity University.

Neustupny, J. V. (1986). Language and society: The case of Japanese politeness. In J. A. Fishman, A. Tabouret-Keller, M. Clyne, B. Krishnamurti, & M. Abdulaziz (Eds.), *The Fergusonian Impact: In honor of Charles A. Ferguson, Volume 2: Sociolinguistics and the sociology of language* (pp. 59–71). Berlin: Mouton de Gruyter.

Neustupny, J. V. (1987). *Communicating with the Japanese*. Tokyo: The Japan Times.

Neustupny, J. V. (1989). Nihonjin no komyunikeeshon koodoo to nihongo kyoiku [Japanese communicative behavior and Japanese language teaching]. *Nihongo Kyoiku* [Journal of Japanese Language Teaching], *67*, 11–24.

Nishida, C. (1981). Ga to wa: Shinjoohoo to Kyujoohoo [*Ga* and *wa*: New information and old information]. *Sophia Linguistica*, *8/9*, 164–173.

Niyekawa, A. M. (1977). Code switching in a stable relationship: An analysis of a Japanese TV drama. *Proceedings of the symposium on Japanese sociolinguistics* (pp. 151–180). San Antonio, TX: Trinity University.

Niyekawa, A. M. (1984). Analysis of conflict in a television home drama. In E. L. Krauss, T. P. Rohlen, & P. T. Steinhoff (Eds.), *Conflict in Japan* (pp. 61–84). Honolulu: University of Hawai'i Press.

Noda, M. (1981). *An analysis of the Japanese extended predicate: A pragmatic approach to the system and pedagogical implications.* Master's thesis, Cornell University.

Noguchi, R. R. (1987). The dynamics of rule conflict in English and Japanese conversation. *International Review of Applied Linguistics in Language Teaching*, *25*, 15–24.

Ogino, T. (1989). Taisho shakaigengogaku to nihongo kyoiku: Nikkan no keigoyoohoo no taishokenkyu o rei ni shite [Constrastive sociolinguistics and Japanese language education: In case of contrastive study of Japan-Korea honorific usage]. *Nihongo Kyoiku* [Journal of Japanese Language Teaching], *69*, 47–63.

Ogino, T., Misono, Y., & Fukushima, C. (1985). Diversity of honorific usage in Tokyo: A sociolinguistic approach based on a field survey. In R. R. Mehrotra (Ed.), *Sociolinguistic surveys in South, East, and Southeast Asia* (pp. 23–39). Berlin: Mouton.

Ohama, R. & Marui, I. (1983). Japanische Interaktionsstrategien: Datensammlung zu einem Programm kontrastiver Untersuchung Japanisch-Deutsch [Japanese interaction strategies: Collection of data for a program of contrastive studies of Japanese and German]. *Studies in Language and Literature*, *3*, 35–133.

Okabe, R. (1983). Cultural assumptions of East and West. In W. B. Gudykunst (Ed.), *Intercultural communication theory: Current perspectives* (pp. 21–44). Beverly Hills: Sage.

Okazaki, T. (1987). Danwa no shido: Sho, chuukyuu o chuushinni [A curriculum for teaching discourse: Focusing on the elementary and intermediate level]. *Nihongo Kyoiku* [Journal of Japanese Language Teaching], *62*, 165–178.

Okushi, Y. (1990). Misunderstood efforts and missed opportunities: An examination of EFL in Japan. *Penn Working Papers in Educational Linguistics*, *6* (2), 65–72.

Ooishi, H. (1979). Keigo ga tadashiku tsukaemasu ka? [Can you use honorific expressions appropriately?]. *Gengo Seikatsu* [Language Life], *295*, 42–49.

Otsuka, Y. (1989). Shiten ni yoru nichi-ei hikaku [Empathy-based differences between English and Japanese]. *Nihongo Kyoiku* [Journal of Japanese Language Teaching], *67*, 173–180.

Reynolds, K. A. (1985). Female speakers of Japanese. *Feminist Issues*, (Fall), 13–46.

Reynolds, K. A. (1987). *Linguistic reflexes of changing relationship between women and men in Japan*. Paper presented at the Third International Interdisciplinary Congress on Women, Dublin, Ireland.

Reynolds, K. A. (1987). *Linguistic reflexes of social stratification: Reference terms in major Japanese newspapers*. Paper presented at the Modern Language Association annual meeting, San Francisco.

Reynolds, K. A. (1989). Gengo to sei yakuwari [Language and sex roles]. In National Women's Education Center (Ed.), *Joseigaku koza* [Women's Studies Lectures] (pp. 61–65). Tokyo: Daiichi Hoki.

Reynolds, K. A. (1989). Josei zasshi no kotoba [Language in women's magazines]. In T. Inoue (Ed.), *Josei zasshi wo kaidoku-suru* [Decoding women's magazines] (pp. 209–227). Tokyo: Kakiuchi Shuppan.

Reynolds, K. A. (1990). Female speakers of Japanese in transition. In S. Ide, & N. McGloin (Eds.), *Aspects of Japanese women's language* (pp. 1–17). Tokyo: Kuroshio Shuppan.

Reynolds, K. A. (1991). *Westernization and sexism in Asian languages.* Paper presented at the panel of "Language, Culture, and Gender in Asia" at the Third University of Hawai'i Graduate Students' Conference, Honolulu.

Reynolds, K. A. (in press). Frauensprache in Japan: Zur geschlechtsspezifischen Verwendung von Personalpronomina im Japanischen [Women's language in Japan: On the sex-specific use use of personal pronouns in Japanese]. In S. Gunthner, & H. Kotthoff (Eds.), *Geschlecht und Kultur im Gespräch* [Gender and culture in conversation]. Frankfurt: Suhrkamp Verlag.

Robinson, M. (1991). Introspective methodology in interlanguage pragmatics research. In G. Kasper (Ed.), *Pragmatics of Japanese as native and target language* (Technical Report #3) (pp. 29–84). Honolulu, Hawai'i: University of Hawai'i, Second Language Teaching & Curriculum Center.

Rowe, H. M. (1982). An example of discourse analysis: A Japanese radio news item. *Journal of the Association of Teachers of Japanese, 17,* 7–19.

Sakamoto, N., & Naotsuka, R. (1985). *Polite fictions: Why Japanese and Americans seem rude to each other.* Tokyo: Kinseido.

Sakamoto, T., Kozuka, M., Hasatani, M., Kosaki, A., Inaba, M., & Harada, C. (1989). "Nihongo no foorinaa tooku" ni taisuru nihongo gakushusha no hanno [Learners' reactions to Japanese foreigner talk]. *Nihongo Kyoiku* [Journal of Japanese Language Teaching], 69, 120–146.

Sato, M. (1989). Gijutsu kenshuin no tame no nihongo kenshu sanjuujikan koosu e no hi-gengo dentatsu doonyu no kokoromi [Japanese nonverbal communication]. *Nihongo Kyoiku* [Journal of Japanese Language Teaching], 67, 87–98.

Sawyer, M. (1991). The development of pragmatics in Japanese as a second language: The particle ne. In G. Kasper (Ed.), *Pragmatics of Japanese as native and target language* (Technical Report #3) (pp. 85–127). Honolulu, Hawai'i: University of Hawai'i, Second Language Teaching & Curriculum Center.

Shibamoto, J. S. (1983). Subject ellipsis and topic in Japanese. *Papers in Linguistics, 16*, 233–265. Also in S. Miyagawa & C. Kitagawa (Eds.), (1984), *Studies in Japanese language use* (pp. 233–265). Carbondale, IL: Linguistic Research, Inc.

Shibamoto, J. S. (1987). Japanese sociolinguistics. *Annual Review of Anthropology, 16*, 261–278.

Shibamoto, J. S. (1987). The womanly woman: Manipulation of stereotypical and nonstereotypical features of Japanese female speech. In S. Phillips, S. Steel, & C. Tanz (Eds.), *Language, gender, and sex in comparative perspective* (pp. 26–49). Cambridge: Cambridge University Press.

Shigeta, M. (1974). Ambiguity in declining requests and apologizing. In J. C. Condon & M. Saito (Eds.), *Intercultural encounters with Japan* (pp. 193–195). Tokyo: Saimul Press.

Shinoda, E. (1981). Donatory verbs and psychological distance in Japanese. *Sophia Linguistica, 8/9*, 142–151.

Shinoda, E. (1983). Donatory verbs and psychological distance. *Sophia Linguistica, 11*, 198–213.

Smith, R. (1983). *Japanese society: Tradition, self, and the social order.* Cambridge: Cambridge University Press.

Suzuki, T. (1986). Language and behavior in Japan: The conceptualization of personal relations. In T. S. Lebra & W. P. Lebra (Eds.), *Japanese culture and behavior: Selected readings* (revised edition) (pp.142–157). Honolulu: University of Hawai'i Press.

Szatrowski, P. (1985). The use of Japanese tense-aspect for vividness effect and participant tracking in conversations about past experience. *Journal of Asian Culture*, 9, 102–124.

Szatrowski, P. (1986). Danwa no bunseki to kyojuho: Kanyu hyogen o chushin ni [An analysis of conversation and teaching: Invitations]. *Nihongogaku* [Japanese Linguistics], 5, 27–41.

Szatrowski, P. (1987). A discourse analysis of Japanese invitation. *Berkeley Linguistic Society*, 270–284.

Takahashi, S. (1987). *A contrastive study of indirectness exemplified in L1 directive speech acts performed by Americans and Japanese*. Unpublished master's thesis, University of Illinois at Urbana-Champaign, Urbana, IL.

Takahashi, T., & Beebe, L. M. (1987). The development of pragmatic competence by Japanese learners of English. *JALT Journal*, 8, 131–155.

Takahashi, T., & Beebe, L. M. (in press). Cross-linguistic influence in the speech act of correction. In S. Blum-Kulka & G. Kasper (Eds.), *Interlanguage pragmatics*. New York: Oxford University Press.

Tamori, I. (1977). NP and particle deletion in Japanese discourse. In E. O. Keenan & T. L. Bennett (Eds.), *Discourse across time and space*. Los Angeles: Department of Linguistics, University of Southern California.

Tanaka, N. (1983). Nihongo kyoiku to danwa no kenkyu [Teaching Japanese language and the study of discourse]. In Kokuritsu Kokugo Kenkyusho [National Language Research Institute] (Ed.), *Danwa no kenkyu to kyoiku I* [The study of discourse in teaching Japanese I] (pp. 113–133). Tokyo: Okurasho Insatsukyoku.

Tanaka, N. (1988). Politeness: Some problems for Japanese speakers of English. *JALT Journal*, 9, 81–102.

Tanaka, N., Aneha, H., & Kawahigashi, I. (1986). Gaikokujin no nihongo koodoo: Kikitori no komyunikeeshon sutoratejii [Foreigners' language behavior in Japanese: Communication strategies in listening]. *Gengo Seikatsu* [Language Life], *418*, 62–71.

Tanaka-Bardin, S. (1986). Japanese as second language: A syllabus for research students. *Sophia Linguistica*, *10/11*, 321–331.

Taniguchi, S. (1989). Kaiwa kyoiku no shirabasu zukuri ni mukete [Preparing syllabuses for teaching conversation]. *Nihongo Kyoiku* [Journal of Japanese Language Teaching], 68, 259–266.

Tatematsu, K. (1989). Gaikokujin gakushusha no Taiguu hyogen no reberu no tekiseisa ni tsuite [On the politeness level]. *Nihongo Kyoiku* [Journal of Japanese Language Teaching], 69, 36–46.

Tokunaga, M. (1988). A paradox in Japanese pragmatics. *IPrA Papers in Pragmatics*, 2, 84–105.

Tsuchihashi, M. (1983). The speech act continuum: An investigation of Japanese sentence final particles. *Journal of Pragmatics*, 7, 361–387.

Tsujimura, T. (1989). Taiguu hyogen (toku ni keigo) to nihongo kyoiku [Taiguu hyogen (attitudinal expressions) and Japanese language education]. *Nihongo Kyoiku* [Journal of Japanese Language Teaching], 69, 1–10.

Tsuruta, Y., Rossiter, P., & Coulton, T. (1988). *Eigo no social skill: Politeness systems in English and Japanese*. Tokyo: Taishukan Shoten.

Ueda, K. (1974). Sixteen ways to avoid saying "no" in Japan. In J. C. Condon & M. Saito (Eds.), *Intercultural encounters with Japan* (pp. 185–195). Tokyo: Saimul Press.

Wenger, J. R. (1983). Some universals of honorific language with special reference to Japanese. *Dissertation Abstracts International*, *43*, 2338-A.

Wenger, J. R. (1983). Variation and change in Japanese honorific forms. *Papers in Linguistics*, *16*, 267–301. Also in S. Miyagawa & C. Kitagawa (Eds.), (1984), *Studies in Japanese language use* (pp. 267–301). Carbondale, IL: Linguistic Research, Inc.

Wetzel, P. J. (1988). Are "powerless" communication strategies the Japanese norm? *Language in Society*, *17*, 555–564.

Yabar, P. (1975). Sobre la particula japonesia *wa* en el habla femenina [On the Japanese particle *wa* in women's speech]. *Lenguaje y Ciencias*, *15*, 89–96.

Yamagiwa, J. K. (1965). Language as an expression of Japanese culture. In J. W. Hall & R. K. Beardsley (Eds.), *Twelve doors to Japan* (pp. 186–221). Maidenhead: McGraw-Hill.

Yamamoto, A. Y. (1983). Presuppositional culture spaces: Language use in everyday life. *Papers in Linguistics*, *16*, 303–349. Also in S. Miyagawa & C. Kitagawa (Eds.), (1984), *Studies in Japanese language use* (pp. 303–349). Carbondale, IL: Linguistic Research, Inc.

Yamamoto, F. (1989). Taiguu hyogen to shite no buntai [The appropriate use of polite plain-form]. *Nihongo Kyoiku* [Journal of Japanese Language Teaching], *69*, 77–92.

Yamanashi, M. (1974). On minding your p's and q's in Japanese: A case study from honorifics. In M. W. LaGaly, R. A. Fox, & A. Bruch (Eds.), *Papers from the tenth regional meeting of the Chicago Linguistics Society* (pp. 760–771). Chicago, IL: Chicago Linguistic Society.

Yamanashi, M. (1989). Pragmatic functions of sentence and text coordination in natural language: A case study of Japanese coordinate expressions. *Text*, *9*, 291–305.

Yamaoka, M. (1989). Shooryaku ni okeru gengogai joohoo no dentatsu [On the communication of deictic information in conversations in which ellipsis occurs]. *Nihongo Kyoiku* [Journal of Language Teaching], *67*, 99–110.

Yamashita, H. (1989). Nihongo kyoiku ni okeru shokyu to taiguu hyogen [Taiguu hyogen (language consciousness) and Japanese language teaching on the elementary level]. *Nihongo Kyoiku* [Journal of Japanese Language Teaching], 69, 11–23.

Yamashita, M. Y. (1983). An empirical study of variation in the use of honorific forms in Japanese: An analysis of forms produced by a group of women in an urban setting. *Dissertation Abstracts International, 44,* 1780-A.

Yokota, A. (1986). Homerareta toki no hentoo ni okeru bokokugo kara no shakaigengogakuteki teni [Sociolinguistic transfer from the native language in the responses to compliments]. *Nihongo Kyoiku* [Journal of Japanese Language Teaching], 58, 203–223.

Yoshikawa, C. (1988). Bamen no sukuriputo to shoryaku gensho [Situational script and ellipsis]. *Nihongogaku* [Japanese Linguistics], 7, 64–76.

Yoshizawa, N. (1981). *Hanashi kotoba to keigo* [Spoken language and honorific expressions]. Tokyo: Kokubungaku Kaisohan.

Yoshizawa, N. (1988). Keigo wa jissai ni wa doo tsukau ka?: Hanasu [How are honorific expressions actually used?: Speaking]. In Kokubungaku Henshubu [Japanese Literature Editorial Board] (Ed.), *Anata mo keigo ga tadashiku tsukaeru* [Even you can use honorifics correctly] (pp. 59–97). Tokyo: Gakudosha.

Mary Ann Robinson

INTROSPECTIVE METHODOLOGY IN INTERLANGUAGE PRAGMATICS RESEARCH

INVESTIGATING PRAGMATIC COMPETENCE

IN RECENT YEARS discussions of communicative competence have included, in addition to linguistic and grammatical knowledge, the notion of pragmatic knowledge. Pragmatic knowledge is seen to interact with other knowledge types – discourse, semantic, grammatical, phonological, sociocultural, and world knowledge – with language users combining elements from all of these to achieve communicative goals (Kasper, 1989b). Pragmatic competence, which is needed in order to accomplish this combination, is defined by Koike as "the speaker's knowledge and use of rules of appropriateness and politeness which dictate the way the speaker will understand and formulate speech acts" (1989, p. 179).

As recognition of the role of pragmatic knowledge in communicative competence has grown, an increasing amount of second language research attention has focused on how non-native speakers (NNS) comprehend and produce speech acts, and how they acquire second language speech act knowledge (Kasper & Dahl, 1991). An important result of interlanguage (IL) pragmatic research in the last ten years has been the documentation and analysis of speech act performance by NNS from a variety of language backgrounds (Kasper, 1989b; Kasper & Dahl, 1991). This body of cross-cultural speech act information has led to a growing understanding of the use of pragmatic knowledge in second language behavior.

Descriptive studies of interlanguage speech act realization have also provided insight into the IL speech act variability which is inherent

Robinson, M. (1991). Introspective methodology in interlanguage pragmatics research. In G. Kasper (Ed.), *Pragmatics of Japanese as native and target language* (Technical Report #3) (pp. 27–82). Honolulu, Hawai'i: University of Hawai'i, Second Language Teaching & Curriculum Center.

in learners and situations, and is also induced by data collection instruments (Kasper, 1989b, Kasper & Dahl, 1991). The results of IL pragmatics research to date suggest that such investigations can reveal substantial insight into the acquisition of second language pragmatics, as well as into the processes of second language acquisition in general.

IL pragmatics research results also help language teachers to direct learner attention to pragmatic concepts and to identify areas where socially appropriate language use is problematic for second language learners. Classroom-based research, such as Kasper's (1989a) investigation of discourse regulation procedures, suggests the value of "metacommunicative activities that raise the learners' consciousness about which discoursal forms, function and procedures are language- and context-specific, and which can be employed most profitably across languages and contexts" (p. 224). Schmidt (in press) makes a similar connection between research and teaching: "Explicit teacher-provided information about the pragmatics of the second language can also play a role in learning, provided that it is accurate and not based solely on fallible native speaker intuitions." Koike (1989) suggests that adult second language learners already have a conceptual framework for polite speech act performance, but that they require guidance in linking L1 rules of appropriate use with those of the L2.

Research into pragmatic competence has for the most part compared the results of cross-cultural investigations into language use (see, for e.g., studies cited in Blum-Kulka, House, & Kasper, 1989). Far fewer studies have examined the processes by which pragmatic competence is acquired (see for e.g., studies cited in Kasper & Dahl, 1991). While product investigations do help to characterize states of IL pragmatic development, performance data give little insight into the language processing that accompanies speech act production. It is this processing which must be examined in order to learn about how second language pragmatic competence is acquired, and about its characteristics at particular developmental stages.

IL pragmatics analysis has tended to rely on three research methodologies; role play, discourse completion tasks (DCTs), and metalinguistic judgement tasks, such as paired comparisons, card sorting, and rating scales (Kasper & Dahl, 1991). Although interviews have also been used in a few research designs, IL pragmatics research has generally based its descriptions of language use on an analysis of learner performance rather than on an examination of cognitive processes. It is the purpose of this paper to investigate the effective use of introspective research methods in producing information about the cognitive processes that accompany second language speech act performance.

INTROSPECTIVE METHODS

Introspective methods have been used in psychological research since the late 1800s. Although largely abandoned during the heyday of behaviorism, introspection has received renewed interest as a means of examining language processing strategies since the 1970s (Börsch, 1986; Ericsson & Simon, 1987).

In second language research, introspection attempts to reconstruct learner interlanguage from verbal reports about how learners solve language tasks in real time. While it may not be possible to determine precisely what happens inside the mind during such processing, asking language users about what they are thinking as they make language decisions is increasingly seen as a valid means of gaining more direct access to the conscious language processing and knowledge which is stored in short-term memory. According to this view, introspection helps to overcome some of the limitations, such as researcher inference about the causes of behavior, which are inherent in performance observations (Gerloff, 1986). Used with a separate data collection tool, introspection also yields insight into language processing unavailable from a single methodological perspective, at the same time enhancing the validity of the research results (Börsch, 1986; Færch & Kasper, 1987b; Haastrup, 1987).

It appears that introspection can also reveal information about language learners' subjective theories about language and learning. Grotjahn (1991) reasons that learners' subjective theories, or aggregates of cognitions that are both relatively stable and potential causes of action, may influence shorter-term cognitions about specific language tasks. If this is so, then investigation of learner theories about language and learning could contribute to an understanding of how second language learners process information related to specific language tasks. Citing research evidence that planning and monitoring strategies play an important part in second language learning and are also partly accessible to introspection, Grotjahn calls for application of subjective theory research to the field of sociolinguistic and pragmatic knowledge.

Defining Introspection

Introspection, verbal reports, and thinking aloud are all terms which are used in the research literature to describe learners' self-reports about language processing. While the meaning of each of these terms has a somewhat different history (see Börsch, 1986; Ericsson & Simon, 1987), each is used here in a specific sense. In this discussion, introspection and introspective methods describe the methodology as a whole and include the more specific notions of verbal reports and thinking aloud. The term "verbal reports" refers to the contents of utterances which are either concurrent with the subject's language processing or delayed until processing is completed. This concurrent/delayed contrast is reflected in Ericsson and Simon's distinction between "concurrent verbal reports ... where the cognitive processes, described as successive states of heeded information, are verbalized directly," and "the retrospective report ... [where] a durable (if partial) memory trace is laid down of the information heeded successively while completing a task" (1984, p. 16). The terms "concurrent" and "retrospective" are adopted here to distinguish reports about on-line processing from accounts of processing which has been completed. Finally, "thinking aloud" is used to describe the simultaneous verbalization of concurrent thoughts.

Introspective methods are believed to produce valid data on the cognitive processes used in problem-solving because, according to memory and information processing models (see Ericsson & Simon, 1984, pp. 11-24), information which is being attended to or which has recently come to a subject's attention is still available for verbal reporting. Therefore, verbal reports about attended input can provide insight into the cognitive processes relevant to that information, with concurrent reports yielding the most valid data. Conversely, information which is not consciously processed cannot be reported. Ericsson and Simon were chiefly concerned with verbal reports as primary data in psychological experimentation, and their model is used to predict problem-solving processes in that field. The research reported here uses essential features of Ericsson and Simon's model to demonstrate the applicability of their research framework to studies of IL pragmatics.

Verbal Reports in Second Language Research

Since introspective methods have been little used in pragmatics research, a discussion of these techniques must initially include second language investigations which do not focus on pragmatics. These studies have examined learner strategies in reading (Block, 1986; Cavalcanti, 1987; Hosenfeld, 1984), writing (Cohen, 1991), lexical inferencing (Haastrup, 1987), test-taking (Feldmann & Stemmer, 1987; Grotjahn, 1987), compensatory strategies (Poulisse, Bongærts & Kellerman, 1987), and translation (Dechert, 1987; Færch & Kasper, 1986; Gerloff, 1986, 1987; Hölscher & Möhle, 1987; Krings, 1986, 1987; Lörscher, 1986; Tirkkonen-Condit, 1986). A description of the use of introspective methods in the few available IL pragmatics investigations (Takahashi & DuFon, 1989; Eisenstein & Bodman, 1986) follows.

Studies of second and foreign language reading have used verbal report procedures to identify reading processes, describe the nature of reading problems, and discover learner strategies for comprehending text (Cavalcanti, 1987; Block, 1986; Hosenfeld, 1984). A second language writing investigation applied both concurrent and retrospective techniques to a study of written teacher feedback on student compositions (Cohen, 1991). This study tape-recorded teachers thinking aloud while they wrote comments on compositions, recorded student reactions to this feedback, and surveyed both teachers and students by questionnaire.

An investigation of hypothesis formation and knowledge sources in second language lexical inferencing also combined concurrent and retrospective data collection techniques (Haastrup, 1987). This research used interacting pairs of subjects in order to promote verbalization during the think aloud session, then added retrospective interviews to probe statements which pairs made during their think aloud discussions. Both Cohen and Haastrup employed retrospection to confirm and expand on data gathered during the concurrent sessions.

Examinations of C-test validity (Grotjahn, 1987) and of C-test-taking strategies (Feldmann & Stemmer, 1987) provided additional examples of the combination of think aloud and retrospective techniques in second language research. Noting the numerous problems inherent in test validation, Grotjahn demonstrated that a variety of data sources when used to study the same problem could create a more valid representation of the research object.

A study of the compensatory strategies used by EFL learners to make up for lexical shortcomings in speech production (Poulisse, Bongærts and Kellerman, 1987) combined four tasks, including two picture descriptions, a story re-telling, and an interview in order to obtain a reasonably generalizable picture of the EFL use of compensatory strategies. This investigation established the value of its retrospective data in the identification of compensatory strategies and in the elimination of compensatory strategies which had been incorrectly identified by second party observers.

Finally, introspective research into translation, using non-professional translators (foreign language learners) as subjects (Dechert, 1987; Færch & Kasper, 1986; Gerloff, 1986, 1987; Hölscher & Möhle, 1987; Krings, 1986, 1987; Lörscher, 1986; Tirkkonen-Condit, 1986) has yielded important information about both language comprehension and production. Færch and Kasper point out that non-professional translators have "the methodological advantage that they carry out large parts of their tasks under conscious attention" (1987b, p. 13).

Verbal report research in IL pragmatics has thus far employed retrospection, but not thinking aloud. Furthermore, retrospection has not been systematically employed in research designs that also include performance observations. Nevertheless, existing second language studies do provide some insight into the uses and limitations of introspection in IL pragmatics research, in addition to the substantive information these studies provide about learners' speech act performance.

Takahashi and DuFon (1989) investigated the cross-linguistic influence of indirectness in requests and request responses using role-plays between a researcher and individual subjects. Following the role-plays, each subject listened to a tape-recording of their role-play conversation and identified the communicative intent of particular utterances selected by the researchers.

Eisenstein and Bodman (1986) used informal retrospective interviews to supplement a DCT investigation of English language learners' expressions of gratitude. Although these researchers did not represent their interviews as formal introspective probes, their research is of interest here because it is one of the few pragmatic studies to include any form of retrospection. The affective nature of some of their interview responses (feeling "uncomfortable" or "unsure") support Seliger's (1983) observation that verbal reports are useful for exploring the affective dimensions of language choice.

Limitations of Introspective Methods in Second Language Research

Both linguists and psychologists have identified weaknesses in introspective data. Seliger (1983), for example, limits the use of verbal reports to investigations of language use rather than its acquisition, a restriction which researchers have observed rather closely. According to Seliger, verbal reports represent only conscious processes, and language learning takes place at the unconscious level (although see Schmidt, 1990, for discussion of the role of attention in language learning). Seliger also notes that introspective data analysis is hampered by a researcher's interpretation of verbal performance in terms of a linguistic system which differs from the subject's "underlying references" (p. 189). Seliger does, however, find application for introspective data in the generation of hypotheses and in the study of affective factors in language behavior.

Further criticism is summarized in Cohen (1987, 1991). Here, second language researchers describe mental processes as too complex to be accurately reported (Boring, 1953; Dobrin, 1986). Concurrent reports are claimed to be too dependent on lengthy retrospection for their explication (Boring, 1953), and too easily influenced by both subject and researcher assumptions about what constitutes socially and culturally appropriate data (Bakan, 1954; Dobrin, 1986; Lyons, 1986, all cited in Cohen, 1991). A more recent criticism, pointed out by Færch and Kasper (1987b), is that processing information may be lost from short term memory or rendered inaccurate if subjects must translate their thoughts from one language to another before reporting.

Still other criticisms have targeted procedural weaknesses: a subject's focus on mental processes is believed to change the nature of those processes (Mann, 1982, cited in Cohen, 1991), and verbal report data is viewed as too easily influenced by the instructions given to subjects, by individual subjects' verbal skills (Haastrup, 1987), by data collection instruments, and by data analysis procedures (Olson, Duffy & Mack, 1984, cited in Cohen, 1991).

Ericsson and Simon (1984, 1987), in their discussion of verbal reports in psychological experimentation, have cataloged researchers' objections to introspective data, but, like Cohen, have done so in order to discourage careless administration of introspective research procedures and to promote the planning which will produce valid and reliable results. Both research parties are, in fact, vigorous proponents of introspective research as a source of information about cognitive processes which is unavailable from other sources. The limitations cataloged by Ericsson and Simon include the opinion of some psychologists that introspective data is useless without external validation, that it is incomplete, that it does not correlate with behavioral observations, and that the instruction to verbalize alters cognitions. These psychologists also claim that researcher bias interferes with validity, that results cannot be generalized, and that subjects cannot accurately report the reasons for their inference-based responses. Nisbett and Wilson (1977), in particular, complain that subjects do not recall cognitive processes from memory, but "theorize" instead (cited in Ericsson & Simon, 1984, p. 27).

Controlling Limitations in Second Language Research

Careful planning of research procedures appears to be the most critical factor in obtaining useful introspective data. In order to improve the validity of introspective data, and to reduce methodological influences, Ericsson and Simon discourage the use of retrospective queries that "lead" subjects, that seek information which subjects did not attend, or that elicit generalizations. On the other hand, they encourage probes of task-related processing. They also suggest limiting the time lapse between task completion and retrospective sessions and using video or audio recordings of task performance in order to activate processing traces in short-term memory and remind subjects of their thoughts. Subjects are also not be told in advance that they will be asked to retrospect.

Cohen (1987, 1991) recommends similar precautions for second language investigations, suggesting that retrospective queries probe only attended information in order to avoid modifying processing sequences and thus encourage subjects to make inferences about incomplete memories. Cohen cautions that probes should be used only to complete reports, and not to obtain information that was not processed. Furthermore, tasks should not require excessive effort, and procedural instructions should make task requirements clear. Like Ericsson and Simon, Cohen recognizes the value of introspective data to descriptions of "learner strategies, notwithstanding the controversy regarding their reliability and validity" (1991, p. 35).

Introspection Plus Retrospection. One means of improving reliability and validity has been the combining of concurrent and retrospective techniques. While concurrent and retrospective reports are similar in some respects, including their representation of intuitions about language decisions, the two perspectives also differ. The accuracy of retrospective reports, in particular, suffers from the elapsed time between task performance and learner comment, from the possibility that subjects

---

know in advance about the retrospective session, and from the researcher bias inevitably imposed during interview interactions. Concurrent reports are also subject to researcher bias, although perhaps more subtly, through training instructions, cues to verbalize, and other less explicitly expressed expectations.

The differences between the two introspective approaches suggest that a combination of techniques can reduce overall data limitations and improve the quantity and quality of data, since subsidiary data helps to interpret primary results (Kasper & Dahl, 1991). Concurrent reports, for example, are less influenced by time lapse or by subject anticipation of an interview than are retrospective accounts. Retrospective reports, on the other hand, can clarify incoherent think aloud data and elaborate truncated utterances. Cohen (1991), Haastrup (1987), Grotjahn (1987), and Feldmann and Stemmer (1987), in their supplementation of think aloud data with data from retrospective interviews, provide prime examples of this combination of introspective tools. Unfortunately, neither introspective procedure entirely eliminates the weaknesses of the other, and some limitations (such as researcher bias) might even be compounded by using both procedures in the same research design.

Verbal Reports plus Discourse Completion Tasks. Although Eisenstein and Bodman (1986) appear to be the only IL pragmatics researchers who combine even an informal version of introspection with a DCT, they are not alone in their use of a DCT as a primary data elicitation device. Kasper and Dahl (1991) cite seventeen IL pragmatics investigations which rely on DCTs for the collection of all or part of their data. Because written elicitation procedures impose data limitations of their own, and because a DCT is used in the present study, it is necessary to comment on the use of verbal reports in connection with DCTs. (See Beebe & Cummings, 1985; Kasper & Dahl, 1991 for a thorough review of DCTs in pragmatics research.)

Eisenstein and Bodman (1986) claimed that their use of a DCT gave informants time to plan their responses, reduced the anxiety of face-to-face encounters, and permitted the collection of large quantities of data. It is also likely, however, that a written instrument causes writing fatigue, allows subjects to edit their answers, eliminates traces of interlocutor influence, and elicits less complex responses than would occur in natural speech. Interpreting the influence of a written task on pragmatics research results is not clear-cut; focus on product may be seen as an obstacle to focus on process, or it may be viewed as one of the "activities that involve slow and controlled processing... [which] open the possibility for introspecting on procedural knowledge" (Færch & Kasper, 1987b, p. 12). In research where subjects write at the same time that they make linguistic decisions, rather than after processing has finished, Færch and Kasper's assessment is probably accurate.

In sum, it seems that verbal reports by learners about their language processing can help to characterize stages of interlanguage development for those learners. The success of these investigations depends in part on the role of verbal reports in data collection, on research goals and theoretical bases, and on the care with which the research is conducted. Verbal reports may be used to generate hypotheses in quantitative approaches, or they may constitute the primary data in qualitative designs, data which may or may not be supplemented by observations from other methodological perspectives (Börsch, 1986). In any case, some second language researchers are increasingly confident that verbal report procedures are a useful means of accessing the mental activities associated with language behavior.

So far, introspective techniques have undergone a respectable trial in second language investigations of reading, writing, lexical inferencing, compensatory strategies, test-taking, and translation. Verbal reports have not yet been adequately tested as research tools in interlanguage investigations of speech act knowledge. It seems appropriate, therefore, to undertake further research into the potential contribution of this methodology to knowledge about pragmatics interlanguage.

THE STUDY OF REFUSALS

Refusals in American English are an important target for interlanguage investigation for several reasons: their formulaic structure often makes them difficult for NNSs to negotiate; they require an ability to manipulate indirect utterances; and they vary under the influence of social, cultural, and other variables (Beebe, Takahashi, & Uliss-Weltz, 1990; Rubin, 1983). As Rubin observes, "it is sometimes difficult to recognize a refusal in one's mother tongue ..., nonetheless in many encounters the meaning is clear if one knows how to read or interpret the appropriate signals" (p. 10). It is no surprise, then, that many NNSs, having had little or no instruction in interpreting these signals, have difficulty both interpreting ambiguous refusals and producing refusals appropriate to situations where they are required.

In view of their social importance, what is surprising is that refusals have not received more research attention. As a response to invitations, offers, and requests, refusals have been treated indirectly in the literature on second language requests (see for e.g., Blum-Kulka, 1983). A small number of more recent studies have examined refusals directly, without an intermediate focus on requests. Takahashi and Beebe (1987, cited in Wolfson, 1989) and Beebe, Takahashi, and Uliss-Weltz (1990), have used DCTs to investigate the evidence for pragmatic transfer in Japanese ESL refusals. Both studies conclude that Japanese ESL students transfer L1 rules of speaking, status considerations, and speech formulae. In addition, the more proficient learners in these studies tended to transfer pragmatic knowledge to a greater extent than did the less proficient subjects.

Chui (1990) compared the English language refusal strategies used by both mainland Chinese and Taiwanese ESL subjects with those used by NSs of American English and found that the refusal strategies used by the Chinese and the Americans were generally similar. Chui speculated that these similarities might have been due to possible parallels between Chinese and American refusal patterns, or to the possibility that her Chinese subjects had acquired English language rules of speaking while in the U.S. or from an English teacher in China, thus obscuring potential differences in Chinese and American norms.

Beebe and Cummings' (1985) study of English NS refusals is relevant here, in spite of the fact that it has no NNS component. This study compared authentic NS telephone conversations to data obtained by means of a DCT. The authentic responses were found to be longer, more complex, and more emotional in tone than the DCT responses, showing the influence on data of the DCT. Davidson (1990) also examined only English language data in her study of refusals, but she does so within an extended discourse context, noting the modifications that refusers make when their initial refusal is rejected. Davidson's approach again highlights the influence of data collection procedures on research results; methodologies which isolate speech acts from their discourse context may obscure communicative intent.

The literature on second language refusals emphasizes the role of pragmatic transfer in IL pragmatics development. The first language studies draw attention to constraints imposed on data by research methodology, to the complexity of speech acts, and to the importance of discourse context. While these insights are important to an understanding of the development of pragmatic competence, the focus of these studies on transfer, and their inferring of results from performance observations emphasize the need for further research into the processes that underlie IL pragmatics decision-making. The purpose of the study which follows is to investigate the role of verbal report procedures in eliciting cognitive processing information about refusals in American English. It is the shortage of research into interlanguage refusals as well as the scarcity of information about the processes of IL pragmatics that determines the research focus.

A VERBAL REPORT INVESTIGATION

THE STUDY REPORTED HERE combines three data collection methodologies; a DCT, concurrent verbal reports from a think aloud session, and retrospective interviews, in research which probes the cognitive processes of language learners as they produce refusals in American English: what it is that learners know about American English refusals, and how they access and apply this knowledge in speech act performance. The primary purpose of this research is to evaluate verbal reports as a means of investigating IL pragmatics knowledge. Specific questions asked in this investigation are:

1) Can verbal reports elicit data that helps to characterize language learners' pragmatic knowledge, as well as some of the sources of that knowledge?

2) Does the type of data elicited by verbal reports differ with the learners' language proficiency?

3) What categories of information do verbal reports yield with respect to IL pragmatic knowledge of American English refusals?

It is hypothesized that the introspective data collected in this research will characterize interlanguage stages to a degree, but that learners will be unable to report their knowledge of L2 rules of use completely, and that the quantity and type of information they do report will vary with linguistic proficiency (Casanave, 1988; Wolfson, 1989).

METHOD

Subjects

The subjects in this study were twelve female Japanese graduate and undergraduate students studying in Honolulu, Hawai'i. The subjects were selected from a pool of twenty students who filled out background questionnaires about personal, language, educational, and intercultural experience (Appendix A). All of the selected subjects were native speakers of Japanese between the ages of 20 and 37 who had lived in the United States for periods ranging from three months to three years. Native language, gender, length of residence, and age variables were held as constant as possible in order to highlight differences in the type of information reported by subjects at different English proficiency levels (see Tables 1 and 2).

To focus on differences according to linguistic proficiency, subjects were divided into intermediate and advanced groups, according to TOEFL scores, self-ratings, and researcher estimates of oral proficiency. Intermediate subjects had TOEFL scores between 480 and 530 and advanced subjects, between 587 and 630. Because TOEFL scores are inadequate predictors of pragmatic competence, subject self-ratings and researcher estimates were added to insure that within-group differences were considerably smaller than differences between groups. It was not possible in this study to pretest subjects for oral proficiency, but the nearly 60 point TOEFL differential, coupled with the two subjective judgements, were considered sufficient here.

Materials

The data collection instrument consisted of a six item DCT (Appendix B) specifying the following contexts:

1) You are asked to function as a secretary of your department's student association. ("Student association")

2) Another student wishes to join your study group. ("Study group")

Table 1 : Subject characteristics
Subjects rated "intermediate" by the researcher

subject number	TOEFL score : date	oral proficiency self-rating	residence in U.S.	age
3	523 : 12/90	beginning	1.0 yr.	20
10	517 : 3/90	intermediate	0.5 yrs.	30
11	530 : 9/90	intermediate	0.3 yrs.	36
12	527 : 7/90	advanced	0.3 yrs.	21
13	527 : 11/90	intermediate	0.7 yrs.	30
14	513 : 11/90	intermediate	1.0 yr.	20

Table 2 : Subject characteristics
Subjects rated "advanced" by the researcher

subject number	TOEFL score : date	oral proficiency self-rating	residence in U.S.	age
2	597 : 12/90	intermediate	3.0 yrs.	27
5	587 : 3/90	advanced	2.0 yrs.	31
6	593 : 9/90	intermediate	2.6 yrs.	26
7	607 : 7/90	advanced	2.6 yrs.	25
8	617 : 11/90	advanced	2.5 yrs.	27
9	650 : 11/90	advanced	1.7 yrs.	37

3) A classmate asks you to help her move. ("Moving")

4) A classmate wants to borrow money from you. ("Borrowing money")

5) You are offered a ride by an unsafe driver. ("Unsafe driver")

6) A classmate wants you to lend her your lecture notes. ("Lecture notes")

Subjects were required to write what they would say in conversation to refuse these requests and invitations made by American female classmates. The number of DCT items was held to six in order to limit subject fatigue and thus reduce the number of incomplete responses (Kasper & Dahl, 1991). In order to avoid "leading" subjects, and to elicit their independent thoughts, DCT situations gave only the details necessary to describe situations clearly, and assumed interlocutors did not include close friends or family (Eisenstein & Bodman, 1986). Assumed interlocutor relationships were also stated consistently in terms of sex, status, and social distance in order to focus on differences by subjects' proficiency level, to control the degree to which subjects supplied their own context, and to elicit comparable responses. DCT situations were adapted from authentic refusal instances told to the researcher by native and non-native English-speaking university students.

Procedure
Pilot testing of the research instrument with two English and two Japanese native speakers revealed comprehension difficulties with the verbal reporting instructions. Pilot subjects were confused about what they should report, did not verbalize continuously, and generalized about probable responses under similar circumstances. Two subjects wrote summaries of their thoughts, rather than the text of interactive refusals. To reduce these problems and to draw attention to thought processes, printed instructions and a brief training session were devised. The printed instructions (Appendix C) emphasized the importance of

continuous, comprehensive verbalization. Training sessions reemphasized these points and gave subjects an opportunity to practice. To reduce the cognitive burden of simultaneous translation, subjects were instructed to report in Japanese if that was the language of their thoughts. Neither the instructions nor the training revealed the fact that subjects would be interviewed after completing the DCT.

The research procedures were administered in an office at the University of Hawai'i. One session was conducted at a subject's home. Sessions began with a review of the background questionnaire and a brief training session. The tape-recorded think aloud sessions which followed lasted between 25 and 75 minutes; subjects were allowed to work at their own pace. Immediately after subjects completed the DCT, the researcher interviewed them for 20 to 30 minutes regarding the content of their utterances from the think aloud session, playing back the tape-recording to remind subjects of specific thoughts, and to discourage them from generalizing about hypothetical instances. The interviews also elicited information about knowledge of American English rules of use and about the language of thoughts during the concurrent session. Finally, the retrospective sessions were used to probe subjects' difficulties with the research procedures.

The retrospective probes focused in part on Ericsson and Simon's notions of intentions, cognitions, planning, and evaluations (1984, p. 198). Questions which explored intentions included: What did you intend to say? Why did you say that? Questions which probed cognitions included: What did you notice about the situation? What were you paying attention to at that moment? What were you thinking when you said that? Questions about planning: What did you plan to say? What did you plan to say first, second, etc.? Finally, evaluation questions asked: What were your alternatives? What else could you have said?

Additional questions which probed pragmatic knowledge included: What training or experience made you say that? Where did you learn that? What would you say if the situation occurred in Japan? These probes were intended to complete and clarify the information from the concurrent session reports. Last, methodological probes included: Was the procedure difficult or confusing? Why? Were you able to report all of your thoughts?

Think aloud data was recorded on a Sony TCM5000EV tape recorder using a condenser microphone. The same equipment was used to play back recordings of the concurrent sessions during the retrospective interviews. Interviews were recorded on a Sony WM AF67 Cassette Corder, also using a condenser microphone.

ANALYSIS

Nine categories of verbal report features were identified and coded in the transcripts from this investigation. These categories included noticed, or attended features of the research situation, evidence of utterance planning, evaluation of alternative utterances, indications of pragmatic and linguistic difficulty, statements of knowledge about American English refusals and possible sources of that knowledge, indications of methodological difficulty, and language of thoughts. Proportional interrater agreement of .77 was established by having two ESL graduate students, both trained by the researcher, and the researcher each code one of the transcripts in its entirety.

Attended information corresponded to Ericsson and Simon's "cognitions," a notion which they define as "attention to selected aspects of the current situation" (1984, p. 198). Attended information in this research consisted of the different aspects of DCT situations to which subjects attended in order to formulate their refusals. Utterance planning in this research corresponded to Ericsson and Simon's concept of "planning," or "intermediate constructions to explore sequences of possibilities mentally, easily recognized by conditional constructions like, 'if X then Y and if Z ...'" (1984, p. 198) In this research, planning was evident in subjects' consideration of variously configured input as potential responses to the DCT. Alternative utterances corresponded to Ericsson and Simon's "evaluations," or "explicit or implicit comparisons of alternatives" (1984, p.198). In this research, evaluation of alternatives occurred when subjects compared alternative refusal strategies to DCT situations.

Pragmatic and linguistic difficulties were coded separately from each other to highlight the pragmatic focus of this research. Separate coding also resulted from pedagogic considerations; the two types of difficulty correspond in a general way to the notions of sociopragmatic and pragmalinguistic failure (Leech, 1983; Thomas, 1983). If, as Thomas suggests, sociopragmatic and pragmalinguistic difficulties require different treatment in the second language classroom, then it seems reasonable to recognize the two types of pragmatic difficulty as separate categories in this investigation as well. Pragmatic difficulty was coded in cases where subjects expressed uncertainty about the social appropriateness of their linguistic behavior. The label of linguistic difficulty, on the other hand, was applied to instances where subjects expressed difficulty in finding the right word, but no difficulty in evaluating the social situation.

Statements of knowledge about appropriate American English refusals (knowledge statements), and utterances suggesting sources of that knowledge (source statements), were closely related in this data to expressions of pragmatic and linguistic difficulty. Where difficulty verbalizations expressed uncertainty, knowledge statements expressed a learner's belief that her assessment of the situation and her knowledge about how to refuse were essentially correct. Knowledge statements consisted of reports which either stated or implied a subject's belief about the content of appropriate American English refusals. Source utterances were relatively explicit statements reflecting a subject's sense of how or where she acquired her refusal knowledge.

Methodological problems included misunderstanding DCT situations or a preference for accepting rather than refusing the requests and invitations. Problems with the verbalization routine were expressed as failure to understand the instructions, failure to verbalize, inability to recall thoughts from the concurrent session during the interview, or inability to verbalize thoughts completely. The final category of coded features, language of thoughts, referred to the language in which subjects, upon retrospection, said they were thinking during the think aloud session. Further discussion and illustrative examples of each of these categories appear below.

RESULTS

The main results of this study demonstrate that verbal report procedures do elicit specific information about the planning processes used by second language learners as they attempt to formulate socially appropriate refusals in American English. The use of retrospective interviews in this investigation helped to clarify data from the concurrent sessions, although some retrospective reports did not relate directly to stimulus-specific thoughts, and learners were also unable to report their complete knowledge about second language rules of use. The DCT data also helped to clarify the introspective data and to draw out differences between what the subjects knew about second language rules of use and their actual speech act performance.

While these results illustrate the incomplete representation of authentic language processes in verbal reports, the incoherent or irrelevant nature of some data, and the occasional tendency for subjects to theorize about their reasons for responses, these results also challenge claims that the instruction to verbalize disrupts thought processes and that verbal report results are too idiosyncratic to generalize. Verbal reports are shown to be a practical means for both generating and investigating hypotheses about second language acquisition of pragmatic knowledge.

Attended Information

Attended information in this data was both subject-internal, that is, retrieved from long-term memory or produced by some inferential process, or subject-external and perceived as an external stimulus, such as a feature of the DCT. Both types of attended information were reported spontaneously in utterances from the concurrent sessions, as well as elicited by the retrospective probe, "what did you notice about this situation?" Instances of attended information were easily identified in these protocols. Two examples are given here, the first from an intermediate and the second from an advanced subject's transcript:[1]

[1]Examples are presented as follows: DCT data first, then concurrent data, displayed as an unbroken block of text, and finally, interview data, marked "R" and

DCT example 1 ("Unsafe driver"):
Thank you very much, but I am not sure whether I can go. I don't need to your help. Thank you.

Concurrent report:
>mm [R: *what are you thinking?*] -- mm here it's not so - cl - cloud - crowded in the road in comparison to Tokyo - so [laughs] - but is the - maybe her driving is terrible

Retrospective report:
>R: *what did you notice about this situation? what was important to you there - that helped you decide what to say?*
>S: um - uh - uh - uh this is [R: *okay*] a little bit difficult to uh to imagine unsafe driving [R: *hm*] uh because and when I I get a driver's license - uh at first I'm not a good driver [laughs] and also many of my friends [laughs] is not good at [R: *okay*] driver and the in Tokyo it's much more crowded [R: *hm*] much more dangerous (subject no. 10)

DCT example 2 ("Unsafe driver"):
OK. Thank you very much. I'll try to find the place and tell you. Do you have a map? Let's go now.

Concurrent report:
>[reading item aloud] [laughs] [R: *what are you thinking?*] [laughs] um - I don't care [laughs] unsafe driving [laughs] - at least um -- she - at least sh we - get an accident

Retrospective report:
>R: *what what was important to you here if the unsafe driving was not important? what did you notice about the situation?*
>S: - um - maybe most important thing - at that time is [R: *no this*

"S" for researcher and subject. Researcher reminders to verbalize are italicized and placed in square brackets within the subject's concurrent report. Unintelligible words are represented by a "*", one "*" per word.
Pauses of less than one second are indicated by a single dash [-]. Pauses of one to two seconds are marked by two dashes [--]. Pauses in which the subject was writing are marked by an equal sign [=].

one] to go - to the place - and fortunately she has a car - and --
yeah - and I have yeah yeah actually I have a um - unsafe
driver friend and [R: *hm*] but when she offers - me a ride I -
yeah I thank her and [laughs] - we go together (subject no. 2)

These reports of attended information show what it was that
these subjects comprehended about the situation, what information they
believed was important to resolve the problem, and what related
knowledge they recalled. It is also clear in these examples that while
each subject paid attention to similar aspects of the same DCT stimulus –
unsafe driving – in their initial selection of information relevant to a
response, each subject ultimately arrived at a different DCT response, the
first subject refusing, and the second subject accepting the offer of a ride.

Planning

Nearly every item of each protocol from the think aloud sessions
contained sequences of utterance planning data. Evidence of planning
was less extensive in the retrospective reports, and often appeared there
as summarized or reorganized versions of utterances from the
corresponding concurrent session, a tendency more evident among the
advanced subjects. One example from an advanced protocol
demonstrates this trend:

DCT example 3 ("Lecture notes"):
I don't have it with me now. Well, you may want to ask someone else
because my notes are terrible and I would feel embarrassed to show it to
you. Please ask someone else.

Concurrent report:
well um - for now I should s tell her that - I don't have it with me
- and uh -- um - um - and so that she she will ask somebody else -
hm -- mm [R: *what are you thinking?*] - but um - she may ask again
- what should I say - um - I cannot tell her that I - I I was absent
from the class - I did attend - um - what I'm gonna say - it's really
hard - um - well - how can I refuse - mm - I can I can just - well

I'll just tell her that I don't have it with me - and I have to - tell her that - my - my notes are - are not good - um - it's not sufficient for her - oh okay I I I should tell her that we- she should ask someone else - = um - well - I don't - I have to ex explain that my notes are good - are not good =

Retrospective report:
> R: *what was important about this situation?*
> S: mm - well - I I I don't want to lend a lazy person uh my notes [laughs] [R: *hmm*] but like I said before it's also important to make other people happy - as long as I can do things for them - so - it's it's easy for me to um to to let other people use my notes - but since I have to refuse um - I just have to say that my notes are not good [R: *hmm*] yeah - or uh because in as long as uh - notes go um I - have a hard time no uh writing down what uh what my professor says and stuff so I may need some help from someone so - as long as I can help I'd like to um - let the people use my no see my notes and so that I can expect someone else to help me some some other time (subject no. 6)

In the sample from the concurrent session report, the subject first decided to tell her classmate that she did not have her notes and that the classmate should ask someone else. The subject then repeated part of this plan and added that her own "notes are not good." In the retrospective report, the subject summarized the entire sequence using only the first excuse. At the same time she added more general but related thoughts about her desire to help people but not wanting to encourage their laziness. The think aloud report thus emphasized thoughts relevant to the planning of a refusal, while the retrospective report emphasized the reasoning behind those thoughts. This subject probably recalled a summary of her planning thoughts rather than the entire sequence because of the apparently greater availability of memory for meaning than of memory for the verbatim contents of completed utterances (see Carroll, 1986, p. 201). This subject also appears to have stored information according to some individual moral criteria, evident in the reasoning of her retrospective report.

Alternatives

Evidence for the existence of conceptual and linguistic alternatives in conversation is available in the form of oral self-correction. Laboratory studies have also produced evidence for internal monitoring and editing at the syntactic and semantic level prior to articulation (Carroll, 1986, p. 261). It seems reasonable to assume that language users would consider pragmatic alternatives as well, and these results support this assumption.

The comparison of alternative utterances in this data was often more implicit than explicit, and some alternatives were verbalized without any stated basis for comparison. In other cases, the alternatives being compared were both verbalized, but incompletely, or separated by intervening statements of plans, beliefs, or feelings. Alternatives appeared in roughly equivalent numbers in both think aloud and retrospective reports and across proficiency levels. Two examples of refusal alternatives, the first from an intermediate subject's retrospective report and the second from an advanced subject's concurrent session report, are given below:

DCT example 4 ("Study group"):
I'm sorry. If you join us, maybe we cannot concentrate studying. It's not your fault. I mean two people are enough for studying together.

Concurrent report:
> hm - I think - so many s - I think two people's enough - hm I - I don't think - if more than two ah three people - it's not - not so um - how [laughs] how I can I say - [R: *what are you thinking?*] well - hm - maybe - we cannot concentrate studying - two is enough - =

Retrospective report:
> R: *why were you changing this?* [S: hm] *here at this point you were*

changing your mind [S: ah] *why did you change your mind?*
S: - [whispered: change] -- ah - I try to s at first I try to say - mm you - you are - talkative or something [laughs] [R: *okay*] it's - rude [laughs] [R: *hm*] I think so - I change my mind [laughs] (subject no. 3)

DCT example 5 ("Study group"):
OK. I'll talk to Chris as soon as possible. But you know, one time she said that she would like to work in a small group or just in a pair. So, I'm not sure what she would say. But I'll let you know later.

Concurrent report:
- uh how can I solve this problem - hm - I'll - always - no - to refuse - somebody - for me it's a really hard - yeah - so maybe again I have to think of something - something - maybe goo - good reasons - hm - soo - oh maybe - the best way is just - ah avoid - giving her [laughs] straight answer - uh maybe I - I'd say oh okay I'll talk about it with - Chris - and let you know - then maybe - try to - avoid seeing her [laughs] - then if it doesn't work - maybe - I would say - to - uh - hm - this is hard - maybe I would say - I oh okay I try first then if sh - she still want to join our group I would say - uh - rea m rea feeling I like to work - rather I like to work - with just Chris alone I don't want big group (subject no. 9)

In example no. 4, the intermediate subject explained in her retrospective comments that she had originally planned to tell her interlocutor that she was too "talkative," but then decided against this utterance on the grounds that such direct attribution of negative characteristics to the interlocutor was "rude." In example no. 5, in contrast, it is evident from the advanced subject's concurrent session report that she was more concerned about the social appropriateness of the act of refusing than about the attribution of negative characteristics. For this subject, avoidance of a "straight answer" or even avoidance of the interlocutor appears to be at the core of a socially acceptable response to item no. 2, "Study group". And even if this subject were to tell her "real feelings" and refuse the interlocutor's request to join the study group, she would still avoid referring to the interlocutor's personality as a factor in the decision to refuse. It is clear in these examples that the two subjects considered different criteria in deciding upon socially appropriate responses.

Pragmatic Difficulty

Reports on pragmatic difficulty were found in both think aloud and retrospective data. Pragmatic difficulty reports were considerably more common in intermediate than in advanced subject's protocols, and difficulties experienced by the intermediate subjects were often marked by concerns for the persuasiveness of excuses and for the maintenance of friendly relations (see for e.g., example no. 11). A few intermediate subject's reports also showed some confusion about the applicability of Japanese pragmatic knowledge to American situations, as well as discomfort with customary response patterns learned by girls growing up in Japan. The following example illustrates this unease:

DCT example 6 ("Student association"):
Oh, that sounds good, but I'm afraid I will be busy for my studying next semester. So I can't help you.

Concurrent report:
> this is uh - a good chance to - improve myself - but - still I feel bad to take over this - this kind of work - hmm but - I'm no good at - um - saying no

Retrospective report:
> R: *let me ask you about that - "I'm no good at saying no" - talk about that a little bit - what have you learned about saying no?*
> S: um - saying no?
> R: *umhum - why did you say that?*
> S: - because I haven't never - I I haven't - learned saying no [R: oh] [laughs] - anytime yes yes yes [R: hm] - oh this is our - custom - Japanese custom - uh - um - any time uh - um - my family taught me - uh smile and - modest - and uh - is - the

attitude is to be - not - not say - no - is very uh - good part - to - uh for - women - Japanese women - sometimes [laughs] [R: hm] and - it's easy to control - and we can keep our - our harmony - with - uh many people - if I say no if I - didn't say no [R: hm]- if any time yes - but - actually - inside - um - I'm so confused because I want to say no - [R: hm] but I'm so shy and hesitate to say no - because I'm not - accustomed to saying just saying no (subject no. 13)

Here, the subject explained her self-assessment that she is "no good at saying no" by describing an aspect of her Japanese upbringing; she was taught by her family that a girl should say "yes" – or at least not say "no" – in order to preserve social harmony. The memory of this lesson, and the social responsibility it conveyed, increased this subject's difficulty in making a refusal in a less familiar, American cultural context. Sociopragmatic transfer, then, prompted at least part of this subject's confusion over what to say.

Linguistic Difficulty

There were fewer reports of linguistic difficulty than of pragmatic difficulty in these protocols, and every coded instance was found in an intermediate subject's utterance. Two examples of intermediate subjects' linguistic difficulties follow:

DCT example 7 ("Study group"):
I'm sorry. I wish I could help you. But this weekend, I have to work part-time.

Concurrent report:
hm - I think - so many s - I think two people's enough - hm I - I don't think - if more than two ah three people - it's not - not so um - how [laughs] how I can I say - [R: *what are you thinking?*] well - hm - maybe - we cannot concentrate studying - two is enough - = - [R: *what are you thinking?*] hmm [laughs] I don't know how to - write - hm - I -- I'm so - poor writer in English [laughs] [R: *okay say that - that's a good thought*] hm = -- [R: *what*

are you thinking?] hm [laughs] [R: *every time you pause remember *]
[laughs] I'm just thinking how to express my feeling - but - I don't
have enough vocabularies - of English so - it difficult to write
(subject no. 3)

This subject attributed her refusal difficulties in part to general
lexical deficiencies, presumably in her vocabulary for refusals. A second
example, from a different intermediate subject's transcript, again suggests
vocabulary deficiencies as a partial explanation for refusal difficulties, at
the same time highlighting a specific shortcoming:

DCT example 8 ("Moving"):
I hate to say that I can't help you, but on Sunday I want to study at
libraly, because I should prepare for the term paper. the due date of it is
Tuesday.

Concurrent report:
   [reading aloud] I hate - to say that I I can't - I can't - I can't help
   you - you - but but mm - but I - but - mm on Sunday - on Sunday
   - Sunday - mm - I want - uh on Sunday I will - I will - uh - I
   would I would like - I will - on Sunday - um - um yeah friends
   would like is too polite so uh - I want - okay I sa I want - I want
   to study - to study - um - I want study - at library - library - be
   because I - because I should - should prepare - prepare - for term
   for the term paper - term paper - the - the due date - the due date
   of - of it is on Tuesday - that's all (subject no. 11)

Here, the subject's linguistic difficulty centered on the use of
"would like to" as opposed to "want to." Her statement that "would like
to is too polite" to use among friends (including the assumed
interlocutor) makes explicit one facet of her pragmalinguistic knowledge.
There were other indications of linguistic difficulty in these
transcripts, including pauses and filled pauses, such as "you know," "um,"
and "what shall I say." Although researcher reminders to verbalize
attempted to discourage lengthy pauses, instances of silence longer than

one second, and occasionally two or three seconds were found in several protocols. Retrospective probes revealed that some of these instances marked the translation of thoughts from Japanese into English, a limitation discussed in more detail below. Cavalcanti (1987) has suggested that pauses represent shifts from automatic to controlled processing, and Bialystok (1990) has characterized fluency as a property of high levels of control, or skilled selective attention. Consideration of these explanations for pauses, or their absence, suggests that the intermediate subjects in this study relied more heavily on controlled processing and were less able to direct attention towards relevant information than were the advanced subjects.

Knowledge about American English Refusals

The reliability of both knowledge and source statements is limited by long-term memory factors that do not so severely constrain verbal reports on other categories of processing information. Because of the possibility of subject error in recalling activities from long-term memory, "it is incorrect to infer that [she] actually performed them earlier" (Ericsson & Simon, p. 258). The reliability of knowledge and source reports is also limited by the fact that pragmatic knowledge may not be entirely available for conscious reporting (Schmidt, in press). Not only is some pragmatic knowledge accessed automatically, but much of it may be acquired implicitly (Schmidt). A strong point in favor of using this verbal data to explore pragmatic knowledge is the fact that it was elicited in connection with specific instances of speech act performance, rather than as non task-related memory.

Knowledge statements appeared in these transcripts to the same extent in both learner groups. The characteristics of these statements, however, varied with proficiency. Intermediate subjects expressed a belief that American English refusals are more direct, or more expressive of one's true feelings. Most advanced subjects, on the other hand, suggested that Americans, at least in some situations, would understand the meaning of an indirect refusal or an inconclusive reply. Examples of knowledge statements follow, the first from an intermediate and the second from an advanced subject's transcript:

DCT example 9 ("Unsafe driver"):
Thank you very much, but I am not sure whether I can go. I don't need to your help. Thank you.

Retrospective report:
> S: at first I write down thank you very much but I'm not sure whether I can go [R: hm] then
> R: *why did you say this?*
> S: um in this is a a - a similar to directly translation in Japanese [R: hm] in in the case of Japanese [laughs] see - many people - mm don't - don't asked any more [R: umhum] but - but after that I thought uh this is not enough [R: hm] I should do refuse more strongly
> R: *why did you think it was not enough? [S: uh] what made you think that? - [S: uh] do you know?*
> S: um yeah - maybe in that case I think in in in English - I should do refuse more directly (subject no. 10)

DCT example 10 ("Study group"):
But we don't have any set time to meet with each other. If your time schedule is not flexible, maybe it's difficult for you to join us. I think there are some other study group. Maybe you can ask them, too. If you really want to join us, let me ask the other person.

Concurrent report:
> well I suppose that I don't like that person - um so I think - I will try to - give her some alternatives like - um - well maybe with some reasons like well we are meeting quite irregularly - so I it may be better idea for you to find some other groups.

Retrospective report:
> R: *in Japanese that other person in in that case then [S: mm] would be able to figure out [S: umhm] that you don't want to [S: umhm] do you think that's true in America too? if you use that kind of [S: *]*
> S: not not always - I think in in American it's better to be direct [R: hm] it's better to say - um - you know and I think

Americans don't care [R: hm] I mean - don't mind very much
if - you know - their reque their their request was rejected but
in Japan - if you ask somebody to do something and if the
person - you know - um - just says no [R: umhm] then you fell
like - you're really rejected [R: hm] - and - some people may
take offense out of it (subject no. 7)

Comparison of these two segments recalls example no. 6, where
sociopragmatic transfer made it difficult for an intermediate subject to
formulate a refusal in English. Here, the intermediate subject at first
planned an indirect refusal, transferring her knowledge of Japanese
speech act behavior. She then recalled knowledge about refusals in
English and added to her DCT response the more blunt "I don't need to
your help." In contrast, the advanced subject recalled differences in
appropriate American and Japanese speech behavior but applied only her
American English rules of use.

Sources of Knowledge

Like knowledge statements, source reports in this investigation were
made by learners in both groups and varied with linguistic proficiency.
The following example from an intermediate subject's report reveals
some potential influences on the acquisition of pragmatic knowledge:

DCT example 11 ("Student association"):
Thank you but I'm sorry I want devote in my major field studying next
semester, so I cannot take it.

Concurrent report:
> oh I have a question [R: uhhuh] asks you to take over means uh sh
> she introduce uh job? [R: she wants to give you her job] oh - oh so
> so I have some free time but I don't want to do it but if um I
> refuse it she what she will think

Retrospective report:
> R: why is that important that she is persuaded by a reasonable reason?
> S: uh if I don't - if I don't say any reas any reasonable reason ah

it means uh that I hate her [R: hmm] - mm but I -

R. *is that something you have learned?* - [S: uh] *about American English?*

S: yeah - yeah - [R: hm] in - uh yeah in English conversat conversation class uh we [laughs] learned [laughs]

R: *oh what did they say?*

S: yeah ah - they - teacher teacher teach taught that uh - mention the reason [laughs] [R: oh] and after that um - you you refuse it

R: *okay what did the teacher say? in the class - she said you have to give a reason?*

S: mm no uh but the - examples for conversation is like that (subject no. 11)

In this example, the subject reported the influence of classroom instruction in refusals, particularly of conversational examples that were presented in class. Later information in this transcript suggests that the teacher was an American.

Advanced subject's reports about knowledge sources were less common than intermediate subjects' utterances, and advanced subjects were sometimes unable to remember knowledge sources as well. One example of an advanced subject's recollection of both training and experiential learning is given here:

DCT example 12 ("Borrowing money"):
I guess I can, but you've borrowed money from me many times and haven't returned any. It's not really a lot, but I don't feel good. I'll lend you for today, but please promise to return soon.

Concurrent report:
>well - um -- I - well this is a - this may be a great chance to tell her that - her habit of borrowing money from me - is bothering me - a lot - um - she doesn't

Retrospective report:

> R: *how did you decide what to say* [S: hmm] *what knowledge or experience?*
>
> S: um - well - in Japan I wouldn't I I could I couldn't say that uh you know you you're borrowing money and you're not returning it at all but here it's very important to uh tell the truth you know tell your true feeling - um
>
> R: *why is that? why do you say that? - how did you learn that?*
>
> S: because uh - verbal explicitness is very important in America or in [R: *hm*] western countries
>
> R: *where did you learn that?*
>
> S: um - I I knew in Japan you know from books and stuff [R: *hm*] and I've experienced here [R: *hm*] yeah and I - the same person asked - a girl to uh - let him - um use her car - but [laughs] I saw - I heard this girl saying no you can't I I don't want to [R: *hm*] I I don't think it's a good idea - for me to ah let you use this my car because it's not nec really necessarily - it's not really uh needed and I don't want you to drive my car she said so I thought - saying a true feeling is not a bad idea [R: *hm*] in the States um - but you know this person may feel a little bad but um - no ah just expressing one's idea is very dif important [R: *umhm*] (subject no. 6)

These examples represent the research protocols as a whole in the sense that intermediate subjects generally reported training influences, while advanced subjects, when they noted knowledge sources at all, remarked on inductive learning from experience. In example no. 12, for instance, the advanced subject reported having noticed a specific occurrence of an explicit refusal made by one American to another. From this one observation, she drew the general conclusion about American English refusals that "saying a true feeling," or being direct, "is not a bad idea in the States."

Methodological Difficulties and Language of Thoughts

The final section of this paper analyzes two related methodological difficulties which each shed light on the effective administration of verbal report procedures: difficulties with the DCT or with aspects of the verbalization routine; and difficulties incurred by attempting to verbalize in English. Subjects in both groups reported these problems, with intermediate subjects reporting them most often.

Subject difficulties with the DCT included the inability to picture settings and interlocutors and a preference for accepting requests and invitations. The intent in underspecifying DCT situations was to allow subjects to supply experiential details of their own which would make the situations more realistic, and procedural training encouraged subjects to think along these lines. Unfortunately, some subjects could not readily picture DCT situations, either because they lacked relevant experience or because long-term memory cues in the stimulus were not sufficiently strong (Ericsson & Simon, 1984). At other times, subjects were able to imagine situations, but they did not verbalize their mental images, reducing the comparability of their cognitive processes and utterance products.

More important to this investigation than problems with the DCT, because of their tendency to limit the quantity and quality of introspective data, were difficulties with the verbalization procedures. Of these, the failure to verbalize, the inability to recall thoughts from the concurrent session, and the incomplete reporting of thoughts were the most significant. Failure to verbalize was not as severe a problem as had been anticipated, perhaps because of the training and prompting procedures employed.

Both intermediate and advanced subjects reported having forgotten some of their thoughts from the concurrent session by the time they were interviewed, and both groups reported having difficulty verbalizing their thoughts as quickly as they occurred. This forgetting of thoughts might have been aggravated by the length of the DCT and by the researcher's occasional failure to replay sections of the tape recording from the concurrent session of sufficient length to remind subjects of their thoughts. Difficulty with the simultaneous reporting of thoughts was reported by subjects in both groups, but for intermediate subjects the problem was apparently exacerbated by the need to translate their thoughts into English before thinking aloud. An intermediate subject's report illustrates both the difficulty of simultaneous reporting and the problem of translation (item-specific data is not included):

Retrospective report (post-item "Lecture notes"):

R: *I just want to ask you a couple of questions about the - procedure - um did you get used to it? or did you find it difficult?*

S: it's difficult

R: *is it difficult? why - why is it so hard?*

S: - because - uh - whenever I - talked by myself [R: *umhm*] in silent - I - catch uh -[R: *umhm*]   my feelings as soon as possible [R: *umhm*] - but if I speak - I have to think [laughs] [R: *hm*] yes

R: *is it slower? is that what you mean?*

S: yes slower

R: *okay - did you learn anything?*

S: - yes I did

R: *what did you learn?* [S: laughs] *can you think?*

S: - um - when I try to speak English - just before - I'm thinking - something in Japanese [laughs] (subject no. 13)

Although this subject expressed the difficulty most succinctly, other subjects in both groups suggested in their retrospective reports that the speed of their thought processes made it impossible for them to report their thoughts completely during the think aloud session.

Subjects in this project were instructed to think aloud in Japanese, if that was the language of their thoughts. But in spite of this instruction, there were only two Japanese utterances in the think aloud data, and both of these were highly routinized expressions. Interviews revealed that some intermediate subjects had, at least intermittently, been thinking in Japanese; only one intermediate subject reported to have been thinking in English throughout the think aloud session, and her claim that she had "tried to think in English" suggests that her first thoughts may have been in Japanese. Advanced subjects, in contrast, reported thinking in English during the concurrent sessions in all but one instance. It is likely that the presence of an American researcher and the conduct of research proceedings in English tended to counteract the instruction to think aloud in Japanese.

Clearly, the retrospective identification of the language of thoughts is difficult for second language learners, as the following example from an intermediate subject's transcript illustrates:

DCT example 13 ("Student association"):
I'm sorry, I don't have enough money to lend you. Because I spent a lot of money.

Concurrent report:
> oh - hm it's too - difficult for me [laughs] hm - how can I uh refuse - let me see [laughs] - [R: *what are you thinking?*] hm - I - I - I don't like that kind of - things to do - I'm not so respons I don't have - enough responsibility - hm --

Retrospective report:
> R: *do you remember what language you were thinking in?*
> S: I think - not Jap ah - I'm not sure [R: *okay*] which one is -- maybe I try to translate ah [R: *hm*] - yeah - maybe at first I always think Japanese [R: *hm*] and - I think so [laughs] because I cannot say - English at the same time m when I - thought
> R: *hm so your first thought was in Japanese - do you think? - and then you translated?*
> S: - mm - some easy wor - words I [R: *hm*] I I I can say I'm sorry [R: *hm*] or I don't know how can I say or [R: *hm*] - in that case um - I often use that expression so - mm I don't think - I - thought - Japanese [R: *hm okay*] - but some - difficult - words maybe - at first I thought Japanese [R: *hm*] (subject no. 3)

The elapsed time between thinking aloud about a DCT item and the retrospective probing of those same item-specific thoughts ranged from 25 minutes to an hour. This suggests a need to probe the language of thoughts at intervals during, rather than after the think aloud sessions, in order to improve the reliability of reports.

DISCUSSION AND CONCLUSIONS

THE RESULTS OF THIS INVESTIGATION demonstrate that verbal report procedures do elicit information about language learners' pragmatic hypotheses in the categories of attended information, utterance planning, alternative strategies, pragmatic and linguistic difficulties, pragmatic knowledge, and language of thoughts. It is also apparent that the introspective data collected in this research provides insight into language processing strategies which are not accessible through an analysis of DCT responses alone, and that the combination of think aloud and retrospective techniques enhances the overall informative value of the introspective data. In addition, there is evidence here that introspective data varies qualitatively according to the language proficiency level of the subjects, although the quantity of data was similar for both of the proficiency levels included in this study, and both groups also reported incomplete pragmatic knowledge. Further research might investigate processing patterns for beginning level second language learners to see how these patterns vary from the results reported here. To be effective, such a study would require that subjects be trained in verbal report procedures in their L1 and that they think aloud in their L1 as well, procedures possible only for a bilingual researcher or team of researchers.

While these results contain useful information about interlanguage pragmatics, at the same time they recall some of the limitations of introspective research discussed in detail above. The claim that verbal reports are interpreted according to a different frame of reference than that of the subjects is particularly relevant; in this study the researcher's interpretive framework was both culturally and linguistically unlike her subjects'. Certainly an American perspective had value, but a Japanese point of view would have enlarged upon the interpretative possibilities. An effective research team in future investigations might include native speakers of both of the subjects' first and second languages, in order to improve the likelihood of native language verbalization, and to add depth to an interpretation of utterance products in terms of refusal formulas or politeness variables.

Further verbal report research is needed in order to pursue some of the lines of investigation suggested by this study. Narrowly focused retrospective probes might, for example, yield specific insight into the types of pragmatic information that individual language learners choose to remember. And explicit probes of language processes might uncover correlations between linguistic proficiency and metapragmatic awareness, identify instances of sociopragmatic transfer, or support predictions about second language learner speech act performance in certain types of situations. Verbal report information about learner difficulties in specific situations could be useful in planning the pragmatic instruction learners need in order for them to function effectively in target environments.

Finally, verbal report techniques might be used in classroom investigations of students' pragmalinguistic and sociopragmatic learning experiences, using the research results to generate classroom discussions about pragmatic beliefs. Interview questions in this application might explore the influence of teachers and methodologies, the cultural settings of experiential learning, and features of the learning situation, such as its immediacy, frequency, duration, and intensity. Interview probes could also examine the role of pragmatic transfer, or perhaps test hypotheses about the acquisition of pragmatic interlanguage already in circulation.

While this investigation confirms Seliger's claim that verbal reports are useful for generating hypotheses, these results also show that carefully conducted introspective procedures are a practical means of investigating those hypotheses (Ericsson & Simon, 1987). According to Færch and Kasper, "One major task for SL research is to reconstruct learners' IL development, i.e., to determine their changing states of competence ..." (1987, p. 5). Verbal reports provide a potentially valid and reliable means of contributing to that reconstruction ◆

ACKNOWLEDGEMENT

I would like to thank Gabriele Kasper for her valuable comments on earlier drafts of this paper.

REFERENCES

Beebe, L. M., & Cummings, M. C. (1985). *Speech act performance: A function of the data collection procedure?* Paper presented at the TESOL Convention, New York, April 1985.

Beebe, L. M., & Takahashi, T. (1989). Do you have a bag?: Social status and patterned variation in second language acquisition. In S. Gass, C. Madden, D. Preston, & L. Selinker (Eds.) *Variation in second language acquisition: Discourse and pragmatics* (pp. 103–125). Clevedon: Multilingual Matters.

Beebe, L. M., Takahashi, T., & Uliss-Weltz, R. (1990). Pragmatic transfer in ESL refusals. In R. Scarcella, E. Andersen, & S. Krashen (Eds.), *Developing communicative competence in a second language* (pp. 55–73). Rowley, MA: Newbury House.

Bialystok, E. (1990). Communication strategies: *A psychological analysis of second-language use.* Cambridge, MA: Blackwell.

Block, E. (1986). The comprehension strategies of second language readers. *TESOL Quarterly, 20,* 463–494.

Blum-Kulka, S. (1983). Interpreting and performing speech acts in a second language: A cross-cultural study of Hebrew and English. In N. Wolfson, & E. Judd (Eds.), *Sociolinguistics and language acquisition* (pp. 36–55). Rowley, MA: Newbury House.

Blum-Kulka, S., House, J., & Kasper, G. (1989). Investigating cross-cultural pragmatics: An introductory overview. In S. Blum-Kulka, J. House, & G. Kasper (Eds.), *Cross-cultural pragmatics: Requests and apologies* (pp. 1–34). Norwood, NJ: Ablex.

Börsch, S. (1986). Introspective methods in research on interlingual and intercultural communication. In J. House, & S. Blum-Kulka (Eds.), *Interlingual and intercultural communication* (pp. 195–209). Tübingen: Gunter Narr Verlag.

Carroll, D. W. (1986). *Psychology of language.* Pacific Grove, CA: Brooks/Cole.

Casanave, C. P. (1988). Comprehension monitoring in ESL reading: A neglected essential. *TESOL Quarterly, 22,* 283–302.

Cavalcanti, M. C. (1987). Investigating FL reading performance through pause protocols. In C. Færch, & G. Kasper (Eds.), *Introspection in second language research* (pp. 230–250). Clevedon: Multilingual Matters.

Chui, S. W. (1990). *Thanks, sorry, excuse: Chinese and American refusals in business situations.* Unpublished scholarly paper, University of Hawai'i at Manoa.

Cohen, A. D. (1987). Using verbal reports in research on language learning. In C. Færch, & G. Kasper (Eds.), *Introspection in second language research* (pp. 82–95). Clevedon: Multilingual Matters.

Cohen, A. D. (1991). Feedback on writing: The use of verbal report. *Studies in Second Language Acquisition, 13,* 133–159.

Davidson, J. A. (1990). Modifications of invitations, offers and rejections. In G. Psathas (Ed.), *Studies in ethnomethodology and conversation analysis* (No. 1) (pp. 149–179). Washington, D.C.: International Institute for Ethnomethodology and Conversation Analysis.

Dechert, H. W. (1987). Analysing language processing through verbal protocols. In C. Færch, & G. Kasper (Eds.), *Introspection in second language research* (pp. 96–112). Clevedon: Multilingual Matters.

Eisenstein, M., & Bodman, J. W. (1986). 'I very appreciate': Expressions of gratitude by native and non-native speakers of American English. *Applied Linguistics, 7,* 167–185.

Ericsson, K. A., & Simon, H. A. (1984). *Protocol analysis: Verbal reports as data.* Cambridge, MA: MIT Press.

Ericsson, K. A., & Simon, H. A. (1987). Verbal reports on thinking. In C. Færch, & G. Kasper (Eds.), *Introspection in second language research* (pp. 24–53). Clevedon: Multilingual Matters.

Færch, C., & Kasper, G. (1984). Pragmatic knowledge: Rules and procedures. *Applied Linguistics, 5*, 214–225.

Færch, C., & Kasper, G. (1986). One learner — two languages: Investigating types of interlanguage knowledge. In J. House, & S. Blum-Kulka (Eds.), *Interlingual and intercultural communication* (pp. 211–227). Tübingen: Gunter Narr Verlag.

Færch, C., & Kasper, G. (1987a). *Introspection in second language research.* Clevedon: Multilingual Matters.

Færch, C., & Kasper, G. (Eds.) (1987b). From product to process: Introspective methods in second language research. In C. Færch, & G. Kasper (Eds.), *Introspection in second language research* (pp. 5–23). Clevedon: Multilingual Matters.

Feldmann, U., & Stemmer, B. (1987). Thin__ aloud a__ retrospective da__ in C-te__ taking: Diffe__ languages — diff__ learners — sa__ approaches? In C. Færch, & G. Kasper (Eds.), *Introspection in second language research* (pp. 251–267). Clevedon: Multilingual Matters.

Gerloff, P. (1986). Second language learners' reports on the interpretive process: Talk-aloud protocols of translation. In J. House, & S. Blum-Kulka (Eds.), *Interlingual and intercultural communication* (pp. 243–262). Tübingen: Gunter Narr Verlag.

Gerloff, P. (1987). Identifying the unit of analysis in translation: Some uses of think-aloud protocol data. In C. Færch, & G. Kasper (Eds.), *Introspection in second language research* (pp. 135–158). Clevedon: Multilingual Matters.

Grotjahn, R. (1987). On the methodological basis of introspective methods. In C. Færch, & G. Kasper (Eds.), *Introspection in second language research* (pp. 54–81). Clevedon: Multilingual Matters.

Grotjahn, R. (1991). The research programme Subjective Theories: A new approach in second language research. *Studies in Second Language Acquisition, 13*, 187–214.

Haastrup, K. (1987). Using thinking aloud and retrospection to uncover learners' lexical inferencing procedures. In C. Færch, & G. Kasper (Eds.), *Introspection in second language research* (pp. 197–212). Clevedon: Multilingual Matters.

Hölscher, A., & Möhle, D. (1987). Cognitive plans in translation. In C. Færch, & G. Kasper (Eds.), *Introspection in second language research* (pp. 113–134). Clevedon: Multilingual Matters.

Hosenfeld, C. (1984). Case studies of ninth grade readers. In J.C. Alderson, & A. H. Urquhart (Eds.), *Reading in a foreign language* (pp. 231–249). London: Longman.

Kasper, G. (1989a). Interactive procedures in interlanguage discourse. In W. Olesky (Ed.), *Contrastive pragmatics* (pp. 189–229). Amsterdam: John Benjamins.

Kasper, G. (1989b). Variation in interlanguage speech act realization. In S. Gass, C. Madden, D. Preston, & L. Selinker (Eds.), *Variation in second language acquisition: Discourse and pragmatics* (pp. 37–57). Clevedon: Multilingual Matters.

Kasper, G. (1990). Linguistic politeness: Current research issues. *Journal of Pragmatics, 14*, 193–218.

Kasper, G., & Dahl, M. (1991). Research methods in interlanguage pragmatics. *Studies in Second Language Acquisition, 13*, 215–247. Also in *Technical Report #1*, Honolulu, Hawai'i: University of Hawai'i, Second Language Teaching & Curriculum Center.

Koike, D. A. (1989). Pragmatic competence and adult L2 acquisition: Speech acts in interlanguage. *The Modern Language Journal, 73*, 279–289.

Krings, H. P. (1986). Translation problems and translation strategies of advanced German learners of French (L2). In J. House, & S. Blum-Kulka (Eds.), *Interlingual and intercultural communication* (pp. 257–269). Tübingen: Gunter Narr Verlag.

Krings, H. P. (1987). The uses of introspective data in translation. In C. Færch, & G. Kasper (Eds.), *Introspection in second language research* (pp. 159–176). Clevedon: Multilingual Matters.

Leech, G. N. (1983). *Principles of pragmatics*. London: Longman.

Lörscher, W. (1986). Linguistic aspects of translation processes: Towards an analysis of translation performance. In J. House, & S. Blum-Kulka (Eds.), *Interlingual and intercultural communication*. Tübingen: Gunter Narr Verlag.

Nisbett, R. E., & Wilson, Timothy D. (1977). Telling more than we can know: Verbal reports on mental processes. *Psychological Review, 84*, 231–259.

Poulisse, N., Bongærts, T., & Kellerman, E. (1987). The use of retrospective verbal reports in the analysis of compensatory strategies. In C. Færch, & G. Kasper (Eds.), *Introspection in second language research* (pp. 213–229). Clevedon: Multilingual Matters.

Riley, P. (1989). Well, don't blame me! On the interpretation of pragmatic errors. In W. Olesky (Ed.), *Contrastive pragmatics* (pp. 231–249). Amsterdam: John Benjamins.

Rubin, J. (1983). How to tell when someone is saying "no" revisited. In N. Wolfson, & E. Judd (Eds.), *Sociolinguistics and language acquisition* (pp. 10–17). Rowley, MA: Newbury House.

Schmidt, R. W. (1990). The role of consciousness in second language learning. *Applied Linguistics, 11*, 129–158.

Schmidt, R. W. (in press). Consciousness, learning and interlanguage pragmatics. In G. Kasper, & S. Blum-Kulka (Eds.), *Interlanguage pragmatics*. New York: Oxford University Press.

Seliger, H. W. (1983). The language learner as linguist: Of metaphors and realities. *Applied Linguistics, 4*, 179–191.

Takahashi, S., & DuFon, P. (1989). *Cross-linguistic influence in indirectness: The case of English directives performed by native Japanese speakers*. Unpublished paper, University of Hawai'i at Manoa.

Takahashi, T., & Beebe, L.. (1987). Development of pragmatic competence by Japanese learners of English. *Journal of the Japan Association of Language Teachers, 8*(2), 131–155.

Thomas, J. (1983). Cross-cultural pragmatic failure. *Applied Linguistics, 4*, 91–112.

Tirkkonen-Condit, S. (1986). Text type markers and translation equivalence. In J. House, & S. Blum-Kulka (Eds.), *Interlingual and intercultural communication* (pp. 95–113). Tübingen: Gunter Narr Verlag.

van Dijk, T. A. (1977). Context and cognition: Knowledge frames and speech act comprehension. *Journal of Pragmatics, 1*, 211–232.

Wolfson, N. (1989). *Perspectives: Sociolinguistics and TESOL*. Rowley, MA: Newbury House.

APPENDIX A

Background Questionnaire

INVESTIGATING AMERICAN ENGLISH REFUSALS
STUDENT BACKGROUND INFORMATION

The following *confidential* information will help me to select subjects who match a particular background profile. Your answers are voluntary, but complete information will help to insure the success of this research. *Participation as a subject in this project will take about an hour of your time. Individual research sessions will be scheduled during Spring Break, 1991, or during some other, mutually convenient time.*

Name _____

Local Address _____

Telephone _____(day) _____(evening)_____

Graduate Student _____ Undergraduate _____Age _____ Sex _____

Major field(s) of study _____

Country of origin _____Native language _____

Other languages that you know (besides English) and estimated level (*beginning*,

intermediate, or *advanced*):

Language   Level

_____   _____

_____   _____

_____   _____

How long have you been in the U.S. (total, if on different occasions)? _____

What other countries have you visited or lived in (**for more than three months**)?

Country name   Length of time there

_____   _____

_____   _____

_____   _____

What percentage of your time in the U.S. have you lived in:

_____ a dorm room?

_____ an apartment or house?

_____ other housing? Please describe: _____

What percentage of your housing arrangements in the U.S. have been:

_____ single/living alone?

_____ shared? Usually with how many other people? _____

What percentage of your free time in the U.S. do you spend with:

_____ Japanese native speakers?

_____ American English native speakers?

_____ Other language speakers? Language(s)? _____

How many semesters have you been at the University of Hawaii?_____

Have you attended other colleges or English language programs in the U.S.?_____

Where?_____

For how many semesters altogether?_____

Please estimate your English language level (*beginning*, *intermediate*, or *advanced*):

_____ Oral

_____ Writing

_____ Reading

If you have attended the University of Hawaii English Language Institute, please note the

highest level ELI courses you have completed:_____

_____

Date of most recent TOEFL test?_____ TOEFL score at that time?_____

Please return this form to my mailbox in the ESL Office (Moore 570) as soon as possible. If you cannot return the form to Moore Hall, call me and I will pick it up from you. If you have any questions, call me at XXX-XXXX (home) or XXX-XXXX (work).
THANK YOU VERY MUCH!

APPENDIX B

Discourse Completion Task

Name _____   Date _____

1. An American classmate who is graduating asks you to take over her responsibilities as secretary of the student association in your department for the next semester. You have some free time, but you do not want to do it.

Classmate: *I really need to find someone soon to take over as secretary of our student association for next semester. You'd be perfect. Could you possibly do it?*

You: _____

_____

_____

_____

_____

2. You and a friend have formed a study group to prepare for the final exam in a difficult class. An American classmate asks you if she can also join your group. You do not want to work with this particular student.

Classmate: *I understand that you and Chris are studying together. I'm having some real problems in this class and and I wonder if I could join you? It would sure help me.*

You: _____

_____

_____

_____

_____

3. An American classmate is moving out of the dorm and into an apartment over the coming weekend. She has a car but she needs your help carrying things and getting organized. You have some free time, but you do not want to help.

Classmate: *I was wondering if you could give me a hand moving this weekend, either carrying stuff or just helping me get unpacked and organized. I've got so much to do in just two days, I could really use your help.*

You: _____

_____

_____

_____

_____

4. You are meeting an American classmate at Burger King to study for a class. She often asks you if she can borrow some money to buy coffee. You have the money but you do not want to lend it to her.

Classmate: *I don't think I brought any money with me. Do you think I could borrow just enough for coffee? I'll pay you back next time.*

You: _____

_____

_____

_____

5. An American classmate offers you a ride to an off-campus meeting which you are both required to attend. You are planning to go, and you need a ride, but you do not want to ride with her because of her unsafe driving.

Classmate: *Since we're both going to that meeting downtown on Thursday, why don't you ride with me? I'd like some company and besides, you could help me find the place we're supposed to go.*

You: _____

_____

_____

_____

6. An American classmate sometimes sleeps late and misses a class that you share with her. This happened again today and she asks if she can borrow your lecture notes. You have the notes but you do not want to lend them to her.

Classmate: *I missed class again today. Do you think you could lend me your lecture notes? I'm really getting behind in that class and I'd sure appreciate your help!*

You: _____

_____

_____

_____

Verbal Report Instructions

INVESTIGATING AMERICAN ENGLISH REFUSALS

Each of the items on the next two pages describes a situation involving American and Japanese female students at the University of Hawaii. Your task is to put yourself in the role of the Japanese student in each situation and decide what you would say in order to **refuse** the request the American student has just made. This is the procedure you will follow:

1. First, read the situation. Remember that the person making the request is an **American female classmate.**

2. Think about what you would say in order to **refuse** the request. Imagine that these are real situations in your daily life and plan a real refusal.

3. *At the same time that you are thinking* about what you are going to say, *speak all of your thoughts aloud into the microphone* . Do not wait until you have finished thinking, but speak your thoughts immediately as they occur. This is called *Thinking Aloud.* Your spoken thoughts should include everything you are thinking about while you decide what to say to the classmate.

4. Say *everything* you think as soon as you think it. Do not revise your thoughts for the tape recorder. If you think in Japanese, say your thoughts aloud in Japanese, too.

5. When you have decided what to say, begin to write your answer in the space provided (following the word "You"). It is difficult to *think aloud* and write at the same time, so do not try to speak your thoughts while you are writing.

6. Remember to think aloud *every time you pause* in your writing. If you change your mind about what you want to say while you are writing, *immediately speak aloud* all of your thoughts about the change.

7. Take your time and **do not** worry about grammar, spelling, or handwriting. Please ask me if you have **any** questions about this procedure. You may also ask questions if you do not understand something on the questionnaire.

8. Most importantly – *keep talking and say everything you are thinking!*

EXAMPLE:
Last year you helped to organize the graduation party for your department. This year the student in charge of organizing the party, an American classmate, wants you to help out again. You have some free time, but you do not want to help.

Classmate: *The party was so successful last year, I want to get the same people to help organize this year's party. I'd really appreciate it if you could help us out again.*

You: _____

_____

_____

_____

_____

Mark Sawyer

THE DEVELOPMENT OF PRAGMATICS IN JAPANESE AS A SECOND LANGUAGE: THE SENTENCE-FINAL PARTICLE *NE*

INTRODUCTION

THE JAPANESE SENTENCE-FINAL PARTICLE *NE* is likely to be one of the first items that a complete stranger to the Japanese language will notice upon eavesdropping on a few Japanese conversations. Its occurrence is extremely frequent, and because it is stressed and often followed by a pause, it is also relatively salient. Yet it is mastered by few learners of Japanese as a second language (JSL). This paper will explore this seeming contradiction by surveying the relevant research to date on the nature of *ne* and its acquisition by Japanese children; then after considering how the issues involved fit into the perspective of interlanguage (IL) pragmatics, it will report on a longitudinal pilot study probing how beginning JSL learners actually progress in their acquisition of *ne*. Although there will be no attempt to explain the learners' degree of acquisition of *ne* in terms of the specific instruction they received, some general pedagogical implications of the observed data will be considered.

LINGUISTIC BACKGROUND

Makino and Tsutsui's (1986) *Dictionary of Basic Japanese Grammar* gives the following rudimentary definition of *ne*: "a sentence-final particle that indicates the speaker's request for confirmation or agreement from the hearer about some shared knowledge." According to Makino and Tsutsui, whether it is confirmation or agreement that is sought depends on the emotive content of the proposition that *ne* follows, and is represented in the intonation of *ne* — falling for agreement and rising for confirmation. Although this distinction works in many cases, it seems

Sawyer, M. (1991). The development of pragmatics in Japanese as a second language: The particle *ne*. In G. Kasper (Ed.), *Pragmatics of Japanese as native and target language* (Technical Report #3) (pp. 83–125). Honolulu, Hawai'i: University of Hawai'i, Second Language Teaching & Curriculum Center.

that a more accurate distinction could be made in terms of expectations. As in the case of English tag questions, falling intonation generally means a stronger expectation for agreement than rising intonation, regardless of the type of proposition. Also of interest in Makino's and Tsutsui's work is their characterization of the distinction between *ne* and *nee*: in their view the second variation occurs simply when the speaker is excited about the content of her sentence.

The more detailed account of *ne* in Martin's (1975) *Reference Grammar of Japanese* begins like this: "The particles *ne[e]* and *na[a]* soften a statement and invite confirmation on the part of the hearer." He likens their use to English "*don't you think...*" and French "*n'est-ce pas?*" Martin attributes the use of *non-final ne* primarily to women and to telephone conversations; he also asserts that overuse of this type of *ne* can be irritating to the listener, and he reports on an interesting social movement apparently active at the time he wrote his book: the *Ne-Sa-Yo Tsuihoo Undoo*, or "Movement to Banish *Ne, Sa, and Yo*". Now, over 15 years later, it seems that these protectors of the language have made little progress. An additional non-final use of these particles described by Martin is the use of *ne[e]* and *na[a]* as interjections, spoken to equals or inferiors, with a meaning roughly comparable to English "*Say...*" or "*Look...*" or "*Hey...*". Martin also speculates on the origin of these particles, commenting that the currently most credible possibility is that *ne[e]*, *na[a]*, and *no[o]* all started as abbreviations of the negative *nai*. If so, this would serve as another demonstration of the affinity of *ne* with English tag questions. Much of Martin's analysis is derived from the dissertation research of Uyeno (1971), which will be discussed next.

RESEARCH ON THE FUNCTIONS OF *NE*

In the context of her discussion of the role of sentence particles in Japanese modality, Uyeno (1971) divides Japanese sentence(-final) particles into two categories: 1) particles expressing the speaker's insistence on forcing the propositional content of the sentence on the hearer; and 2) particles giving the hearer the option of confirming agreement or compliance with the utterance's propositional content. *Ne* and its variants comprise the second category, and have the effect of softening the basic nature of each sentence type. Since they show consideration of the hearer and facilitate the hearer's involvement in the conversation, Uyeno calls them "particles of rapport."

Kamio (1979), in contrast, argues for a cognitive rather than affective function for *ne*. In his analysis, *ne* serves primarily to mark information as belonging to the hearer's "territory of information," as opposed to that of the speaker. In other words, *ne* signals metaknowledge on the part of the speaker concerning the sharedness of information between her and the hearer; information supposed to be new to the hearer, therefore, should not be marked by *ne*.

Oishi (1985) analyzes the use of sentence-final particles by videotaping a reunion of family and old friends, and then using the participants' own reactions to a playback of the videotape to get a more complete picture of the functions that the particles served in the conversation. Oishi finds that Kamio's (1979) concept of territories of information also seems to fit his data well, but that the distinction needs to be broadened from a binary to a three-way distinction, between information belonging to the hearer, information belonging to both hearer and speaker, and information belonging to the speaker only.

Ishikawa (1988), working with a database of (personal) written correspondence, examines *ne* within the context of a many-to-many relationship between form and function. Although not seriously taking issue with Kamio's basic argument that *ne* serves primarily a cognitive function, she finds that Kamio's proposal can account for less than 50% of the occurrences of *ne* in her corpus. Ishikawa thus prefers a multifunctional explanation of *ne* along the lines of the scheme provided by Schiffrin (1987), with no core meaning but with primacy still attributed to the cognitive function of marking the field of information.

Among important studies not focusing specifically on sentence-final particles but relevant to the present study are Hinds (1978) and Maynard (1989). Hinds' research sheds light on both the interview as a format for data collection, and on the nature of Japanese conversation. Unfortunately, it is not easy to tell exactly where the light is being shed, since Hinds conflates the two features in one set of data. One very interesting finding, nevertheless, is that extended instances of overlapping speech are quite common in Hinds' interviews, in apparent violation of both sociolinguistic (e.g. SacksSacks, Schegloff, & Jefferson 1974) and neurobiological (Jaffe & Feldman 1970) constraints; another is that the speakers' efforts toward mutual accommodation and creation of solidarity bonds go far beyond what could be accomplished through choice of address terms and levels of formality. He attributes this accommodation to the Japanese quest for empathy in conversation. For the present study, what is especially useful is Hinds' corroboration in interviews of various characteristic features of Japanese conversation reported by other researchers using other data collection procedures.

The largest in scale and the most carefully controlled study on Japanese conversation to date is that of Maynard (1989), who examines a variety of features, including sentence-final particles, in relation to "self-contextualization," which she defines as "the ongoing process of defining oneself in relation to one's interactional environment."[1] Using videotaped quasi-natural conversations among friends (with the researcher not present), she argues that the frequent use of propositionally vacuous sentence-final particles by interactants helps to intensify the level of involvement of the participants, and that their sensitivity to varying levels of involvement constitutes an important part of the self-contextualization process.

Another important aspect of Maynard's study is the introduction of the Pause-bounded Phrasal Unit (PPU) as a unit of analysis for Japanese conversation. Noting that Japanese conversation tends to be fragmented into units even smaller than Chafe's (e.g. 1985) "idea units," in that they are often verbless, she also finds that in her data these units are frequently followed by particles (such as *ne*) which function to elicit listener response. In fact, 30% of the sentence-final particles in her data

---

[1]Self-contextualization consists of two interacting stages: 1) 'contextual interpretation,' which involves "the participant's understanding of actual signs and other abstract structural and interactional knowledge labeled as 'elements of conversation'"; and 2) 'contextual transformation,' which "requires the participant to process his or her ideas and intentions in such a way as to suit each situation of talk by 'transforming' information to conform with the context."

occur at a PPU boundary but not sentence-finally. Only slightly over half occur sentence-finally, with another 19% occurring internally within PPUs. In sum, Maynard's work highlights both the pervasive nature of interactionally-oriented particles in Japanese conversation, and their importance in actually defining the nature of the ongoing discourse.

Although Maynard emphasizes the affective nature of the process of self-contextualization, the most explicitly affect-oriented (and also the most parsimonious) explanation of the particle *ne* is that argued by Cook (1990). Drawing on groundbreaking work on the relationship between language and social categories by Fillmore (1975), Levinson (1983), Silverstein (1976), and Ochs (1988), Cook proposes that all uses of *ne* include the direct indexing of "affective common ground," whereas various social relationships and other conversational functions are indirectly indexed according to the interactional context. Using natural data primarily from 16 hours of audiotaped family dinner conversations with no researcher present, Cook demonstrates how previous accounts of *ne* emphasizing agreement or territory of information are inadequate on their own but can be easily incorporated into her framework of direct and indirect indexicality.

To bolster her interpretation of *ne*, Cook elaborates on the central role that affective common ground plays in Japanese conversation, explaining how the Japanese take the creation and maintenance of affective unity to be an important goal of conversation. In addition to various forms of crosslinguistic and anthropological evidence, she derives the most explicit empirical support for her position in the findings of Hinds (1978) on extended overlapping of speech and Maynard (1989) on frequent head movements and back channel expressions, as well as her own and others' work demonstrating the pervasiveness of *ne*. Also relevant to the present study is Cook's assertion, backed by informal evidence, that it is difficult for Japanese to carry on conversation without the use of *ne*.

With some perspective on the problems that scholars of Japanese have had in characterizing these non-obligator particles, it is time to turn to the acquisition of these particles by Japanese children, which turns out to be not much of a problem at all.

ACQUISITION OF SENTENCE-FINAL PARTICLES

Clancy's (1986) survey on the L1 acquisition of Japanese focuses on an evaluation of Slobin's (e.g. 1973) universal operating principles, which entail cognitive constraints on a child's perception and production of speech, and on how a child organizes and stores linguistic rules. Nevertheless, she finds that her Japanese data demonstrate a crucial role for affect and pragmatic development in the early stages of language acquisition. Although early sensitivity to affect probably contributes to the development of intonation in all languages, Japanese has many grammatical forms, including sentence-final particles such as *ne*, whose appropriate use depends largely on a sensitivity to how they relate to attitude and feelings. Clancy offers evidence to show how the acquisition of negation, polite verb forms, and pronouns for first and second person reference require this competence, concluding that "although affect probably plays a major, as yet unexplored, role in the acquisition of all languages, Japanese children will find more obvious and consistent grammatical correlates of their emotions than children acquiring many other languages." (p. 511)

Clancy goes on to discuss the role of presupposition, which is crucial to the acquisition of sentence-final particles, as *yo* typically presupposes that new information is being conveyed, whereas *ne* often presupposes shared information. Since the appropriate use of these particles seems to require the child's recognition of how her state of knowledge and/or attitude compares with that of the hearer, an interesting question arises regarding the supposed egocentrism of young children: if they are so egocentric, how are they able to generate the necessary insights into the hearer's point of view? Clancy goes no further than to suggest additional research on this, but it seems plausible that the nature of the particular language and language-specific relationship between speaker and hearer may accelerate the development of the capacity for presuppositions. Furthermore, a child's socialization into a particular speech community may condition her view about the amount and type of presupposing that is expected in language, a conditioning that could lead to problems when learning an L2.

Finally, in her suggestions for future study, Clancy proposes that since some, but not all, Japanese particles are plurifunctional, a longitudinal contrastive analysis of their acquisition would provide an interesting test case for Slobin's hypothesis that children prefer a one-to-one mapping of form and meaning. She also suggests that since the languages most thoroughly studied to date do not have the extensive overt morphological expression of emotional and pragmatic functions comparable to those served by Japanese sentence-final particles, additional research on these particles should provide valuable insights into the roles of affect and presupposition in the earliest stages of language acquisition.

Although Clancy's (1986) paper mentions the early acquisition of *ne*, Clancy (1987) goes into much more detail. Two important considerations relevant to *ne*'s role in Japanese conversation emerge. The first is that the use of *ne* typically occurs when mothers are also expressing positive affect through other means, and therefore *ne* is acquired early quite likely due to this association with positive affect. The second is that its development is likely to be strongly influenced by the linguistic empathy training that mothers give their children, inculcating sensitivity to the needs, wishes, and feelings of others. Thus, Clancy illustrates a situation in which socialization and language acquisition seem to be intertwined very harmoniously.

A question which logically follows here is how different from this is the picture with adult JSL learners?

INTERLANGUAGE PRAGMATICS

Blum-Kulka, House, and Kasper (1989), in their introductory overview to the field of cross-cultural pragmatics, make the case that interlanguage pragmatics remains underdeveloped in comparison with either contrastive pragmatics or interlanguage studies of phonological, morphological, and syntactic knowledge. Although interest in interlanguage pragmatics increased throughout the eighties, it is still the case that nonnative speech act performance has been investigated almost exclusively in just two languages (English and Hebrew), and with a focus on communication rather than learning (some of the few exceptions are Scarcella and Brunak 1981, Olshtain and Blum-Kulka 1985, Trosborg 1986, and Svanes in press). Thus Blum-Kulka et al. make the case that more developmental studies, and more studies of a wider range of L2s, are badly needed in IL pragmatics. A methodologically-oriented update on studies in interlanguage pragmatics, Kasper and Dahl (1991), shows that a wider variety of languages are represented as either L1 or L2 in some of the most recent work in interlanguage pragmatics, and that different proficiency levels are being used, but that a true focus on the acquisition of L2 pragmatics is still lacking.

Although there are apparently no previous studies dealing specifically with IL pragmatics in Japanese, one piece of research relevant to the present study is an investigation of the input that IL Japanese speakers receive. Hiraike-Okawara and Sakamoto (1990) investigated the modifications made by Japanese native speakers (NS) in conversations (informal interviews) with learners of Japanese, in comparison with the same native speakers' conversations with their Japanese friends. Specifically, they looked at modifications in the range of vocabulary used (type/token ratio) and differences in word class distribution. Unexpectedly, they found that the type/token ratio was higher in "foreigner register," and they also found this type of speech to be characterized by avoidance of interrogative pronouns, honorifics, adverbs, and sentence-final particles, in contrast to an overabundance of proper nouns, numerals, –masu verb forms, and grammatical (case and topic marking) particles. Of particular interest here is that ne/na occurred four times more frequently in NS-NS conversation than in NS-NNS conversation, even though both kinds of dyads could be considered to constitute in-group relationships (NSs were close friends or host families of the NNSs). The authors explain this result by speculating that the NSs presumed these pre-intermediate NNSs not to know those particles, which are often associated with informal speech. This principle of avoiding features of informal speech would also fit the relatively heavy use of the polite *–masu* verb forms in "foreigner register," and the inclusion of grammatical particles which are normally dropped by NSs.

IL SPEECH ACT REALIZATION AND
SENTENCE-FINAL PARTICLES

In the interlanguage realization of various speech acts, Thomas (1983) argues that there are two types of pragmatic breakdown that can occur. The first type, pragmalinguistic, occurs when the IL speaker simply uses a linguistic realization that NSs would not generally use for that speech act; the second type, sociopragmatic, occurs when the realization of the speech act indicates to the NS hearer that there is a mismatch between the hearer's and the speaker's perception of some aspect of the social relationship between them. Although the distinction between the two types can sometimes be blurred, problems of either type in the realization of familiar speech acts tend to be discrete and identifiable, and therefore are arguably accessible to recognition and restructuring by the learner. Something as plurifunctional and ubiquitous though non-obligatory as Japanese sentence-final particles, on the other hand, present a more complex learning problem for the learner, and communication problems until they are learned. There is no single speech act that cannot be performed without *ne*, yet it may be that the full range of speech acts will be rendered less successful if *ne* and other particles are not used appropriately. Even when learners realize this fact, they will generally find it difficult to determine to what extent they are using affective particles adequately, since native speakers, often unable themselves to pinpoint problems when they exist, will not be able to provide useful feedback.

THE STUDY

PURPOSE

THIS STUDY SEEKS to make a start toward understanding the development of pragmatic competence in Japanese as a second language (JSL), by chronicling the development of the sentence-final particle *ne* in one group of JSL learners over the period of one year. It represents one approach to analyzing the rich corpus of JSL data collected by the staff of the Japanese Language Program (JLP) of the International University of Japan (IUJ), as part of the University of California Pacific Rim Research Project. Though a number of data elicitation instruments were devised and implemented by IUJ's JLP staff to investigate a wide variety of JSL acquisitional phenomena, this study limits itself to only one language feature (*ne*), and analyzes only one type of data (that gathered through semi-structured interviews). It is hoped that the results will be suggestive of areas where future JSL pedagogy might fruitfully concentrate its efforts.

RESEARCH QUESTIONS

To what extent do JSL learners manage to acquire sentence-final particles? Are any particular developmental sequences involved? Do learners receiving the same instruction tend to show similarities in their use of these particles, or are their clear differences among them? Answers to these questions should shed some light on the communication and learning problems surrounding sentence-final particles in Japanese. The analysis will focus on the particle *ne*, both because of its importance, and because the other particles are too infrequent in the data to analyze.

Based on the disagreement evidenced by scholars, the particle's minimal contribution to referential communication, and the anecdotal evidence of numerous JSL teachers and learners, it is possible to offer some very tentative hypotheses to help focus the study.

HYPOTHESES

1) The development of *ne* will lag behind both general vocabulary development and the development of grammatical particles.

2) The use of *ne* will occur at first primarily in fixed phrases learned as chunks, gradually spreading to a limited number of more productive contexts.

3) There will be a large amount of individual variation among learners on this feature.

SUBJECTS

Subjects were beginning students in the IUJ Japanese Language Program, learning Japanese to enrich their stay in Japan while they completed a two-year English-medium Master's degree course in either International Relations or International Management. Many were also anticipating the need to use Japanese in the positions they hoped to secure upon graduation. Although over 30 students participated in the research project, complete sets of data are available for only 11 of them; it is those 11 subjects whose data will be analyzed here. Their native language background breakdown is as follows: Bengali (B)=4; Brazilian Portuguese (BP)=2; Persian (P), British English (E), Hindi (H), Thai (T), Urdu (U)=1 each. In this sample there was only one woman (identified as BP1).

PROCEDURES

The data for this study was collected longitudinally over one year, at four points: 11/89, 2/90, 5/90, and 11/90. Thus the first data collection took place approximately two months after Japanese instruction began. The primary goals of the interview were to draw as much Japanese as possible from the subjects, and to make the interviews, over time and across interviewers, as comparable as possible. To these ends, a structured interview format was agreed upon, whereby a number of standardized questions were asked, concerning, for example, the student's weekend routine or information about her country, but with the interviewer having license to allow the subject to go off in any direction that would generate more learner speech. Interviewers were instructed to facilitate this process with as little of their own speaking as possible. The interviewers were all native speakers of Japanese: five IUJ JLP instructors, one visiting JSL instructor; and one JSL instructor-in-training.

The data was transcribed by native Japanese speakers who were trained for the task, and every transcript was checked by at least one other transcriber. The transcription system roughly followed the guidelines distributed by the University of Hawai'i Center for Second Language Classroom Research. Transcripts were later reformatted by the present researcher to be readable by the computer program CLAN (Computerized Language ANalysis) developed by MacWhinney (1991).

DATA ANALYSIS

The CLAN program was used to calculate frequency of occurrence of *ne* and other relevant items, and the total word types, word tokens, and type/token ratios for each subject; it also was used to isolate the different linguistic contexts in which *ne* occurred. Based on these contexts, it was possible to devise a preliminary categorization of different types of uses for the subjects in this sample. Because of time constraints and the exploratory nature of this pilot study, no inferential statistics were calculated.

RESULTS

Concerning Hypothesis 1 about the slow development of *ne* in relation to general vocabulary development and the development of grammatical particles, it is clear from Tables 1 and 2 this is indeed the case. Table 1 shows that whereas all subjects made rather dramatic gains in the number of different lexical items (types) they used from Time 1 to Time 3, with a more gradual increase to Time 4, the situation with *ne* at Time 3 was that three out of eleven subjects had still not uttered their first *ne*, with three more subjects managing only one occurrence. At Time 4 (six months later), only one subject had still not produced a single *ne*, but the average percentage of occurrences of *ne* to total word types for the group is still very low (2%). Unfortunately, type/token ratio of lexical usage proved unsuitable as an index of general vocabulary development, as the values do not increase consistently as acquisition proceeds. As learners in this data set became more proficient, they produced more speech, but much of the additional speech consisted of more creative and/or appropriate use of previously learned lexical items. Interestingly, the overall type/token ratio for the learners is not substantially lower than that for their NS interviewers (see Table 2).

Table 2 shows the overall occurrences of *ne* in relation to grammatical particles, with the interviewers serving as a basis for comparison. Remarkably, for all of the grammatical particles except *e*, the percentages are not dissimilar for interviewers and subjects. In general, the subjects tend to use grammatical particles a bit more than the interviewers. However, in the case of *ne*, the situation is reversed, with the interviewers using *ne* four times as frequently as the subjects. It should be noted here that in Table 2, the percentages of use of *ne* and other particles are calculated in relation to total word tokens, whereas in Table 1 the percentages were calculated in relation to total word types. This is because Table 1 attempts to depict the use of *ne* in relation to overall vocabulary learning, whereas Table 2 is designed to show the the usage of particles in relation to each other and the interview participants' total speech production.

Hypothesis 2, concerning the sequence of linguistic contexts in which *ne* is used, is also supported by the data. The use of *ne* occurs at first primarily in fixed phrases learned as chunks, gradually spreading to a limited number of more productive contexts. Table 3 shows that at Times 1 and 2, there were too few occurrences of *ne* to see any systematicity in its use in different contexts, but at time 3 the fixed formula, or chunk *soo desu ne*,[2] was clearly the most commonly occurring form. A look ahead to Table 4 shows that *soo desu ne* also had the widest distribution among subjects, with seven of the 11 subjects using it at least once. The next most frequently occurring uses of *ne* were with the copula *desu* not preceded by *soo*, and with other verbs. There is then a dramatic drop in frequency of use of *ne* following nouns and adverbs, uses which are often non-sentence-final. The other typically non-sentence-final position of *ne*, after particles, shows an equally dramatic rise in occurrences in Table 3, but Table 4 shows this reversal of the pattern to be an aberration: all but one of the occurrences of *ne* following particles are produced by one subject.

Hypothesis 3, that individual learners will vary greatly in their acquisition of *ne*, finds substantial support in Table 4. The learners of this sample fall into three groups: one group consists of one learner, U1, whose ability to use *ne* in all linguistic contexts indicates that he is on his way to mastering the productive use of *ne*; a second group consists of three learners, E1, T1, and and P1, who used *ne* 12–15 times each in the data, including in at least three different linguistic contexts; the third category includes the other seven learners, who used *ne* five or fewer times, in 0–3 different linguistic contexts. These are of course very rough categories, and even within them there is much variability in the pattern of acquisition. The most remarkable result is that of U1, who, while being the only learner to use *ne* consistently in non-sentence-final positions, does not appear to use the formulaic expression *soo desu ne* at all. One possible explanation for this unusual pattern is that since *soo desu ne* can usually be replaced by a more specific expression, U1 perhaps tries intentionally as a learning strategy to use the appropriate specific expression.

DISCUSSION

The interview data used in this study demonstrates clearly that a year after beginning their study of Japanese while living in Japan, all of these

---

[2]Also included in this category was its more informal variant, *soo ne*; both of them have a range of meaning roughly corresponding to English: *Right*; *Yeah*; *Yes that's right*; *I agree*; *I hear what you're saying but I don't agree*; *I heard your question and now I'm buying time to formulate an answer*; etc.

Table 1 : Frequency of *ne* in relation to total word types used, by time and subject

Subject ID	Time 1			Time 2			Time 3			Time 4		
	types	ne	ne%	types	ne	ne%	types	ne	ne%	types	ne	ne%
U1	61	0	0%	172	6	3.49%	278	10	3.6%	275	34	1.24%
E1	87	0	0%	189	2	1.06%	215	10	4.65%	178	3	1.69%
T1	163	1	0.61%	177	0	0%	218	8	3.67%	199	4	2.01%
P1	118	0	0%	162	0	0%	211	4	1.9%	250	8	3.2%
H1	128	0	0%	183	0	0%	193	1	0.52%	272	4	1.47%
BP1	123	0	0%	216	0	0%	255	2	0.78%	207	2	0.97%
B2	120	0	0%	221	0	0%	285	0	0%	377	3	0.8%
BP2	138	0	0%	112	0	0%	210	0	0%	244	3	1.23%
B1	153	0	0%	267	0	0%	342	2	0%	182	0	0%
B4	53	0	0%	190	1	0.53%	217	0	0%	244	0	0%
B3	74	0	0%	225	0	0%	187	0	0%	285	0	0%
TOTAL	1218	1	0.08%	2114	9	0.43%	2611	37	1.42%	2713	61	2.25%
MEAN	110.73	0.1	0.06%	192.0	0.82	0.46%	237.36	3.36	1.43%	246.64	5.55	2.16%

Table 2: Overall frequency of *ne* in relation to grammatical particles
(total occurences and as a percentage of the total tokens)

| | Group | | | |
	Interviewers		Subjects	
Total Word Types	1483		3071	
Total Word Tokens	10938		24563	
Type/Token Ratio	0.136		0.125	
	total	%	total	%
ne	242	2.2%	112	0.5%
wa	510	4.7%	1434	5.8%
ga	177	1.6%	447	1.8%
o	181	1.7%	432	1.8%
ni	232	2.1%	589	2.4%
de	149	1.4%	392	1.6%
e	27	0.3%	199	0.8%

Table 3 : Frequency of *ne* by time and linguistic environment (all subjects)

Time	Chunk	Copula +	Verb +	Noun +	Adverb +	Particle +	TOTAL
1	0	1	0	0	0	0	1
2	2	3	4	0	0	1	9
3	14	4	8	1	1	9	37
4	6	8	4	7	7	29	61
TOTAL	21	16	16	8	8	39	108

Table 4 : Frequency of *ne* by linguistic environment and subject

Subject ID	Chunk	Copula +	Verb +	Noun +	Adverb +	Particle +	TOTAL	Non s-final
U1	0	3	3	2	4	38	50	40
E1	5	0	8	0	2	0	15	2
T1	6	5	0	0	1	1	13	4
P1	6	4	1	1	0	0	12	1
H1	0	3	1	1	0	0	5	0
BP1	1	0	0	2	1	0	4	1
B2	1	0	0	2	0	0	3	0
BP2	0	1	2	0	0	0	3	1
B1	2	0	0	0	0	0	2	0
B4	0	0	1	0	0	0	1	0
B3	0	0	0	0	0	0	0	0
TOTAL	21	16	16	8	8	39	108	49

learners have developed a sufficient command of the language to answer questions about themselves and their countries quite adequately; yet it is equally clear from the data that only one of them has developed productive use of the affective particle *ne*, considered by many to be so important in making Japanese conversations flow smoothly. Since learners cannot help but hear the particle *ne* in the input, and probably much more frequently than the grammatical particles which they are producing much more consistently, a large part of the problem may simply be that learners tend to focus on different features, either as a result of predominately grammar-oriented instruction, or of an overriding concern with the referential functions in the second language at the expense of relational functions, or both of the above. As Clancy's studies show, despite the complexity of affective particle usage, *ne* is developed quite rapidly by very young children. Thus it is quite reasonable to expect that adult learners should be able to overcome the obstacles to using these particles effectively, as the learner U1 seems to have, once they appreciate what functions the particles can serve for them in their conversations with Japanese people.

Although no strict developmental sequence can be inferred from these data, for most of the learners in this sample the acquisition of *ne* began with the formulaic expression *soo desu ne*, which is not at all surprising in light of the fact that it is not only frequent and salient in the input, but also extremely useful. It may be only a slight exaggeration to say that a conversational partner, whether Japanese or NNS, can keep a conversation going for quite a while with nothing more than *soo desu ne*. For NNSs, it serves the double role of providing support to encourage the interlocutor to continue speaking (and thus avoid having to formulate a substantial contribution oneself), and filling the silence when it is necessary to formulate a substantial utterance. The other interesting finding is that in terms of frequency, the categories that normally appear sentence-finally (copula + *ne* and lexical verb + *ne*), occurred about twice as often as those which often occur PPU-final but not sentence-final (noun + *ne*, adverb(ial) + *ne*, particle + *ne*). Judging by the pattern of the most successful learner, and weaker indications from the some of the others, a speculation worthy of investigating further is whether the use of *ne* following other particles might serve as a threshold, after which *ne* and other affective particles can be used in a native-like range of linguistic environments.

Concerning individual differences, a look at the Appendices (complete occurrences of *ne*, by linguistic category (Appendix One), and complete occurrences of *ne* by subject (Appendix Two)) will provide clues to many different strategies for using *ne*. The learners tend to use repeatedly the same kinds of phrases, sometimes identical ones, even though, with the exception of *soo desu ne*, each learner's fixed phrases are quite different from those used by other learners. The analysis of a larger sample, with a closer examination of the progression of each interaction between learner and interviewer, should allow these differences to be articulated more precisely.

LIMITATIONS

This study is limited in numerous ways. The learner sample is small and may not be representative of the IUJ JSL population, since the learners who managed to make time for all four data collection sessions are likely to have been the most motivated and/or organized. The learners were from many different L1 backgrounds, sex of subject and interviewer was not controlled for, and no independent evidence was provided to demonstrate that the learners started with the same (lack of) proficiency. The interview format is not a natural situation for gathering conversational data, in that the information exchange is more or less one way, and interviews may be especially unnatural when the interviewers are the subjects' teachers and when the subjects are asked to talk about similar things in each interview. The analysis is limited by assuming that simple numbers of occurrences are a sufficient indication of a learner's state of acquisition of a certain feature; the next stage of analysis will have to attempt to make more sense of the data by using criteria such as "supplied in obligatory context" (SOC) and "target-like use" (TLU). Since inferential statistics are also lacking in this stage, it cannot be verified that any of the quantitative differences that appear to exist are not due to chance.

PEDAGOGICAL IMPLICATIONS

Considering the exploratory nature and limitations of the study, it would not be warranted to base any strong pedagogical prescriptions on the data presented in this paper. Nevertheless, the tentative results produced thus far are suggestive of pedagogical areas which merit additional attention, and are indeed consistent with much recent pedagogical literature and the experiences of both many learners and teachers of Japanese. Although it has become at least somewhat uncontroversial that communicative activities have a place alongside structurally-oriented frontal instruction in the Japanese classroom, the communicative activities that are now used are most often designed specifically to reinforce specific grammar points, or at least to practice certain aspects of referential communication. As was pointed out earlier, however, the importance of Japanese affective particles does not manifest itself openly when the communicative goal is simply the transmission of propositional meaning. Therefore, it would seem fruitful to try to create situations in the classroom in which learners could use language with the principle aim of maintaining smooth relationships with their interlocutors, or to engage in "self-contextualization," in Maynard's (1989) terms.

The deficiencies in learners' communicative competence which can result from an exclusive concern in the classroom on referential aspects of communication are well-documented in Kasper (1989). She shows how learners' over-exposure to "educational discourse" can leave them ill-prepared to deal with many functions which are essential to success in "non-educational discourse." Specifically, Kasper compares the nature of English discourse openings, closings, and regulation in the two types of contexts, illustrating how dramatically the realizations of these functions typically differ according to setting, and showing how violations of conversational rules in non-educational discourse are attributable to learners' lack of exposure to them in the educational discourse of English language classrooms in Germany.

There are at least two reasons to suspect that the situation for classroom learners of Japanese may be even more serious than the one elaborated by Kasper (1989). The first is that openings and closings that she focuses on tend to be highly routinized, whereas the "creating and maintaining affective unity" that Cook (1990) argues to be an important goal in Japanese conversation is a much more pervasive and ever-changing task. Secondly, whereas Kasper's German learners of English had the potential to adapt their L1-based discourse knowledge to the quite similar L2 (although they admittedly had trouble activating this knowledge), many L2 learners of Japanese are likely to take much time before they begin to realize the importance of the affective aspects of communication for the Japanese. And that realization is only the starting point for the development of affectively-oriented pragmatic competence.

Although Japanese instructors may have good reason for emphasizing grammatical competence and the polite, somewhat formal, speech in their classrooms, it should also be clear by now that there also needs to be a place in the syllabus for learners to work on the less formal affectively-oriented conversation which characterizes much non-educational discourse, and which is essential for learners to feel comfortable with if they are going to develop social relationships in Japanese outside of the classroom. Instructors who are fearful that learners will misuse and/or overuse affective particles if they are taught in class should keep in mind that the classroom is the most ideal place for providing feedback on inappropriate usage, feedback which may never be forthcoming at all in the real world.

CONCLUSION

DESPITE THE LIMITATIONS, this study has brought to light some important phenomena which up until now could only be discussed with anecdotes and personal experiences. The development of pragmatic competence in a second language is an area clearly worth serious study, and the Japanese research emphasizing the importance of the speaker-hearer relationship offers additional compelling reasons to proceed in this direction. It is hoped that this preliminary investigation of the acquisition of one pragmatically-sensitive Japanese particle, *ne*, will kindle the imaginations of other researchers potentially interested in this type of research ◆

ACKNOWLEDGEMENTS

The data reported in this paper are from the IUJ corpus of JSL acquisition. Data collection was funded by a grant from the University of California Pacific Rim Research Project, Barry McLaughlin, principal investigator. The corpus was collected by Michael Harrington, UC Santa Cruz, and a research group at the International University of Japan led by Yoshiko Tamaru. Members of the IUJ research group were Shigekazu Hasegawa, Yuutaka Ikeda, Kaoru Yoshioka, Shizuka Kimura, and Rieko Sawyer. The data were transcribed by Reiko Katoh and Aki Suehiro. I would also like to thank Gabriele Kasper, Haruko Cook, Thom Hudson, Michael Harrington, and Kaoru Yoshioka for their valuable comments on an earlier draft of this paper, some of which unfortunately can not be incorporated until the next stage in the research.

REFERENCES

Blum-Kulka, S., House, J., & Kasper, G. (1989). Investigating cross-cultural pragmatics: An introductory overview. In S. Blum-Kulka, J. House, & G. Kasper (Eds.), *Cross-cultural pragmatics: Requests and apologies* (pp. 155–173). Norwood, N.J.: Ablex.

Chafe, W. (1985). Linguistic differences produced by differences between speaking and writing. In D. Olsen, N. Torrance, & A. Hilyard (Eds.), *Literacy, language, and learning: The nature and consequences of reading and writing* (pp. 105–123). Cambridge: Cambridge University Press.

Clancy, P. (1986). The acquisition of Japanese. In D. Slobin (Ed.), *The crosslinguistic study of language acquisition* (pp. 373–524). Hillsdale, N.J.: Erlbaum.

Clancy, P. (1987). *Expression of affect in the acquisition of Japanese grammar.* Paper presented at the 1987 International Pragmatics Conference, Antwerp, Belgium.

Cook, H. (1990). *Meanings of non-referential indexes: A case study of the Japanese sentence-final particle ne.* Unpublished manuscript, University of Hawai'i.

Fillmore, C. (1975). *Santa Cruz lectures on deixis 1971.* Mimeo, Indiana University Linguistics Club.

Hinds, J. (1978). Conversational structure: An investigation based on Japanese interview discourse. In J. Hinds & I. Howard (Eds.), *Problems in Japanese syntax and semantics.* Tokyo: Kaitakusha.

Hiraike-Okawara, M., & Sakamoto, T. (1990). Japanese foreigner register in the use of vocabulary. In O. Kamada & W. Jacobsen (Eds.), *On Japanese and how to teach it* (pp. 211–223). Tokyo: Japan Times.

Ishikawa, M. (1988). *The cognitive and interactional functions of the Japanese sentence particle ne in written discourse*. Unpublished M.A. thesis, the State University of New York at Buffalo.

Jaffe, J., & Feldman, S. (1970). *Rhythms of dialogue*. New York: Academic Press.

Kamio, A. (1979). On the notion of speaker's territory of information. In G. Bedell, E. Kobayashi, & M. Muraki (Eds.), *Explorations in linguistics: Papers in honor of Kazuko Inoue* (pp. 213–231). Tokyo: Kenkyuusha.

Kasper, G. (1989). Interactive procedures in interlanguage discourse. In W. Oleksy, (Ed.), *Contrastive pragmatics* (pp. 189–229). Amsterdam: John Benjamins.

Kasper, G., & Dahl, M. (1991). Research methods in interlanguage pragmatics. *Studies in Second Language Acquisition, 13*, 215–247. Also in *Technical Report #1,*, Honolulu, Hawai'i: University of Hawai'i, Second Language Teaching & Curriculum Center.

Levinson, S. (1983). *Pragmatics*. Cambridge: Cambridge University Press.

MacWhinney, B. (1991). *Computational tools for language analysis: the CHILDES system*. Hillsdale, NJ: Erlbaum.

Makino, S., & Tsutsui, M. (1986). *A dictionary of basic Japanese grammar*. Tokyo: The Japan Times.

Martin, S. (1975). *A reference grammar of Japanese*. Rutland, VT: Tuttle.

Maynard, S. (1989). *Japanese conversation: Self-contextualization through structure and interactional management*. Norwood, NJ: Ablex.

Ochs, E. (1988). *Culture and language development*. Cambridge: Cambridge University Press.

Oishi, T. (1985). *A description of Japanese final particles in context*. Unpublished Ph.D. dissertation, University of of Michigan.

Olshtain, E., & Blum-Kulka, S. (1985). Degree of approximation: Nonnative reactions to native speech behavior. In S. Gass & C. Madden (Eds.), *Input in second language acquisition* (pp. 303–325). Rowley, MA: Newbury House.

Sacks, H., Schegloff, E., & Jefferson, G. (1974). A simplest systematics for the organization of turn-taking for conversation. *Language*, 50, 696–735.

Scarcella, R., & Brunak, J. (1981). On speaking politely in a second language. *International Journal of the Sociology of Language*, 27, 59–75.

Schiffrin, D. (1987). *Discourse markers*. Cambridge: Cambridge University Press.

Silverstein, M. (1976). Shifters, linguistic categories, and cultural description. In K. Basso & H. Selby (Eds.), *Meaning in anthropology* (pp. 112–171). Albuquerque: University of New Mexico Press.

Slobin, D. (1973). Cognitive prerequisites for the development of grammar. In C. Ferguson & D. Slobin (Eds.), *Studies of child language development*. New York: Holt, Rinehart, & Winston.

Svanes, B. (in press). En undersøkelse av realisasjonsmønstret for språkhandlingen "å be noen om å gjøre noen". *Maal og minne*, 3–4.

Thomas, J. (1983). Cross-cultural pragmatic failure. *Applied Linguistics*, 4, 91–112.

Trosborg, Anna (1987). Apology strategies in natives/non-natives. *Journal of Pragmatics 11*, 147–167.

Uyeno, T. (1971). *A study of Japanese modality: A performative analysis of sentence particles*. Unpublished Ph.D. dissertation, University of Michigan.

APPENDIX ONE:
COMPLETE OCCURRENCES OF *NE*
BY LINGUISTIC CATEGORY

CHUNKS (FORMULAIC)

BP1/3[†]   :soo desu NE.

B1/3:   soo desu NE.
B1/3:   soo NE.

E1/2:   soo desu NE.
E1/3:   soo desu NE.
E1/3:   soo NE.
E1/3:   soo NE.

P1/3:   soo desu NE.
P1/3:   soo desu NE.
P1/3:   soo desu NE.
P1/4:   soo desu NE.
P1/4:   soo desu NE.
P1/4:   soo desu NE.

B2/4:   soo desu NE.

[†] subject ID/time

T1/3:	soo desu NE.
T1/3:	soo desu NE.
T1/3:	soo desu NE.
T1/3:	soo desu NE.
T1/4:	soo desu NE.
T1/4:	soo desu NE.

OTHER COPULA

BP2/4:	...sono hitotachi NO yoona onaji desu NE.

P1/3:	desukara [a] zenbu koto WA [a] muzukashii desu NE.
P1/4:	iran WA ookii kuni desu NE.
P1/4:	[a] sotsugyoo shita ato DE totemo [a] ureshii deshita NE.

U1/2:	[aa] watashi no kuni wa [ano] totemo ii kuni desu NE.
U1/2:	ichiban yuumee desu NE.
U1/2:	onaji ja nai desu NE.

H1/4:	shakai NO ii koto desu NE.
H1/4:	demo indo NO ima shakai NO ii koto desu NE.
H1/4:	...watashi WA daitooryoo NI naritai desu NE.

T1/1:	ii ii daogaku desu NE.
T1/3:	tottemo karai desu NE TO ii mashita.
T1/3:	oishii oi– oishii desu NE.
T1/3:	demo tottemo karai desu NE TO iimashita.
T1/4:	tanoshikatta soo desu NE.

OTHER VERBS

E1/2:	takusan no uchi arimasu NE.
E1/3:	furu [ano] toshiyori NO hito hito [ano] takusan mimasu NE.
E1/3:	demo nihon jin WA ichiban ii bunka WA amerika NO bunka TO omoimasu NE.
E1/3:	soshite indo bunka WA takusan NO koto GA arimasu NE.
E1/3:	amerika jin WA kono teepu O kikimasen NE.

E1/3:   soshite [ano] nihonjin TO hanashi nagara narimasen NE.
E1/3:   benkyoo shimasu NE.
E1/4:   [tatoeba NE] [ano] kokusai daigaku DE nihonjin GA ippai
        imasu NE.

BP2/4: demo koko NI kite [a] chotto chigaimasu NE.
BP2/4: ...minna chotto chigaimasu NE.

P1/4:   demo ta [a] tatoeba gohan O tabemasu NE.

U1/2:   sensee wa ie no chotto waruku narimasu NE.
U1/2:   shinbun ga shinbun ga takusan arimasu NE.
U1/3:   [ano] {curry} yori sono WA motto oishii TO omoimasu NE.

H1/3:   sensei WA {x} GA daisuki TO iimashita NE.

B4/2:   shinde imashita NE.

NOUNS
BP1/3: chisai na gakko NE...
BP1/4: mondai NE.

P1/4:   iran NE ...

U1/4:   {BMW} NE...
U1/4:   nanka NE...

B2/4:   TOKA seifu NO shigoto TOKA {politics} NE...
B2/4:   sorede senkyuuhyaku nanajuuichinen NE...

H1/4:   [ano] mono NO mikata mikata NE..

ADVERB(IAL)S
BP1/4:   demo tabun NE...

E1/4:   tatoeba NE sono hito WA watashi NO tomodachi desu.
E1/4:   tatoeba NE [ano] kokusai daigaku DE nihonjin GA ippai imasu
NE.

U1/4:   daitai NE tochi O motteru hito GA.
U1/4:   tokidoki NE [ano] uchi GA kookyoo NO yoo desu.
U1/4:   dakara ima NE itsumo kenka O shite iru [ano] {debate} ?
U1/4:   dakara {x} nakanaka NE.

T1/3:   daitai NE.

PARTICLES
U1/2:   kirei de wa arimasen desu GA NE.
U1/3:   pakisutan WA NE indo TO afuganisutan NO aida NI arimasu.
U1/3:   isuramaWA ano keshiki WA NE [ano] urasa NO keshiki TO
daitai onaji desho.
U1/3:   karachi WA NE.
U1/3:   demo karachi WA NE pakisutan NO ichiban NO kokusai tokai
desu.
U1/3:   ...pakisutan NO tabemono WA NE sekai DE tabun ichiban
oishii tabemono deshoo.
U1/3:   karee yori WA NE.
U1/3:   icchiban tanoshi koto WA NE watashi WA inaka NI sundeiru
koto...
U1/3:   iyankoto WA NE tabun nihon NO tabemono desho.
U1/3:   demo nan WA NE mise KARA mise DE kau pan WA nan
desho.
U1/4:   warui mondai WA NE shite imasen.
U1/4:   ato ima WA NE tabemono [TOKA NE] keshiki NO mono
TOKA...
U1/4:   TOKA NE.

U1/4:   watashi GA sunde iru tokai WA NE
U1/4:   okane P1/ toreru kedo demo {cotton} WA NE momen momen.
U1/4:   yushu shite pakisutan WA NE yushu wata O yushu shite.
U1/4:   pakisutan DE WA NE {BMW} TOKA [a] {BMW} [NE].
U1/4:   zenbu DE NE...
U1/4:   tatoeba indo TO kurabete TOKA NE...
U1/4:   pakisutan WA NE.
U1/4:   kuni WA NE dakara komatte iru.
U1/4:   jibun DE NE jibun DE okane ima tsukutte imasu.
U1/4:   ima igiriru DE NE apaato motte iru hito P1/ imasu.
U1/4:   ato inaka NO hoo GA NE {xxx}. jibun NO [ano] nohara.
U1/4:   hatake O motte inai hito WA NE nanka [NE] koojoo TOKA
      [NE]...
U1/4:   TOKA NE.
U1/4:   demo sore WA NE kuni...
U1/4:   demo sorede WA NE anmari keiken GA {x} nai KARA ii
      shushoo{x}.
U1/4:   ato onaji yoona kangaekata WA NE [ano] anmari yoku nai
      desu.
U1/4:   demo [ano] {mouslim} NO kuni DE NE.
U1/4:   isuramu kyoo NO naka DE NE futatsu guruupu GA aru.
U1/4:   aa suriranka DE WA NE [ano] isuramukoo NI shinjite iru hito
      P1/ iru shi...
U1/4:   demo pakisutan DE WA NE minna shuukyoo WA onaji desu
      keredo [ano] kenka shimasu.
U1/4:   ato hoka NO WA NE...
U1/4:   dakara mae NO shushoo WA NE butto san.
U1/4:   butto san WA amerika DE benkyoo shita koto GA aru hito DE
      NE.
U1/4:   {partly} ajia NO kuniguni WA NE mada dentooteki.
U1/4:   kangaekata WA NE.

T1/4:   iya datta koto WA NE tabun amari suki DE WA nai mono WA
      [a] nihonryoori desu.

APPENDIX TWO:
COMPLETE OCCURRENCES OF *NE*
BY SUBJECT

B1/3[†]:   soo desu NE.

B1/3:   soo NE.

B2/4:   soo desu NE.

B2/4:   sorede senkyuuhyaku nanajuuichinen NE...

B2/4:   TOKA seifu NO shigoto TOKA {politics} NE...

B4/2:   shinde imashita NE.

BP1/3:   chiisai na gakko NE...

BP1/3:   soo desu NE.

BP1/4:   demo tabun NE...

BP1/4:   mondai NE

BP2/4:   ...minna chotto chigaimasu NE.

BP2/4:   ...sono hitotachi NO yoona onaji desu NE.

BP2/4:   demo koko NI kite [a] chotto chigaimasu NE.

E1/2:   soo desu NE.

E1/2:   takusan no uchi arimasu NE.

E1/3:   amerika jin WA kono teepu O kikimasen NE.

[†] subject ID/time

E1/3:	benkyoo shimasu NE.
E1/3:	demo nihon jin WA ichiban ii bunka WA amerika NO bunka TO omoimasu NE.
E1/3:	furu [ano] toshiyori NO hito hito [ano] takusan mimasu NE.
E1/3:	soo desu NE
E1/3:	soo desu NE.
E1/3:	soo NE.
E1/3:	soo NE.
E1/3:	soshite [ano] nihonjin TO hanashi nagara narimasen NE.
E1/3:	soshite indo bunka WA takusan NO koto GA arimasu NE.
E1/4:	(tatoeba NE) [ano] kokusai daigaku DE nihonjin GA ippai imasu NE.
E1/4:	tatoeba NE [ano] kokusai daigaku DE nihonjin GA ippai (imasu NE).
E1/4:	tatoeba NE sono hito WA watashi NO tomodachi desu.

H1/3:	sensei WA {x} GA daisuki TO iimashita NE.
H1/4:	...watashi WA daitooryoo NI naritai desu NE.
H1/4:	[ano] mono NO mikata mikata NE..
H1/4:	demo indo NO ima shakai NO ii koto desu NE.
H1/4:	shakai NO ii koto desu NE.

P1/3:	desukara [a] zenbu koto WA [a] muzukashii desu NE .
P1/3:	soo desu NE .
P1/3:	soo desu NE .
P1/3:	soo desu NE.
P1/4:	...iya datta koto WA nai desu NE.
P1/4:	[a] sotsugyoo shita ato DE totemo [a] ureshii deshita NE.
P1/4:	demo ta- [a] tatoeba gohan O tabemasu NE .
P1/4:	iran NE ...
P1/4:	iran WA ookii kuni desu NE .
P1/4:	soo desu NE .
P1/4:	soo desu NE .
P1/4:	soo desu NE.
T1/1:	ii ii daogaku desu NE.

T1/3:   daitai NE.

T1/3:   demo tottemo karai desu NE TO iimashita.

T1/3:   oishii oi- oishii desu NE.

T1/3:   soo desu NE.

T1/3:   soo desu NE.

T1/3:   soo desu NE.

T1/3:   soo desu NE.

T1/3:   tottemo karai desu NE TO ii mashita.

T1/4:   iya datta koto WA NE tabun amari suki DEWA nai mono WA
         [a] nihonryoori desu.

T1/4:   soo desu NE.

T1/4:   soo desu NE.

T1/4:   tanoshikatta soo desu NE.

U1/2:   [aa] watashi no kuni wa [ano] totemo ii kuni desu NE.

U1/2:   ichiban yuumee desu NE.

U1/2:   kirei de wa arimasen desu GA NE.

U1/2:   onaji ja nai desu NE.

U1/2:   sensee wa ie no chotto waruku narimasu NE.

U1/2:   shinbun ga shinbun ga takusan arimasu NE.

U1/3:   ...pakisutan NO tabemono WA NE sekai DE tabun ichiban
         oishii tabemono deshoo.

U1/3:   demo karachi WA NE pakisutan NO ichiban NO kokusai tokai
         desu.

U1/3:   demo nan WA NE mise KARA mise DE kau pan WA nan
         desho.

U1/3:   icchiban tanoshi koto WA NE watashi WA inaka NI sundeiru
         koto...

U1/3:   isurama WA ano keshiki WA NE [ano] urasa NO keshiki TO
         daitai onaji desho.

U1/3:   iyankoto WA NE tabun nihon NO tabemono desho.

U1/3:   karachi WA NE.

U1/3:   karee yori WA NE.

U1/3:   pakisutan WA NE indo TO afuganisutan NO aida NI arimasu.

U1/3:   [ano] {curry} yori sono WA motto oishii TO omoimasu NE.

U1/4:   aa suriranka DEWA NE [ano] isuramukoo NI shinjite iru hito
        P1/ iru shi...

U1/4:   ato hoka NOWA NE...

U1/4:   ato ima WA NE tabemono [TOKA NE] keshiki NO mono
        TOKA...

U1/4:   ato inaka NO hoo GA NE {xxx}.jibun NO [ano] nohara.

U1/4:   ato onaji yoona kangaekata WA NE [ano] anmari yoku nai
        desu.

U1/4:   butto san WA amerika DE benkyoo shita koto GA aru hito DE
        NE

U1/4:   daitai NE tochi O motteru hito GA.

U1/4:   dakara ima NE itsumo kenka O shite iru [ano] {debate} ?.

U1/4:   dakara mae NO shushoo WA NE butto san.

U1/4:   dakara {x} nakanaka NE.

U1/4:   demo [ano] {mouslim} NO kuni DE NE.

U1/4:   demo pakisutan DEWA NE minna shuukyoo WA onaji desu
        keredo [ano] kenka shimasu.

U1/4:   demo sore WA NE kuni...

U1/4:   demo sorede WA NE anmari keiken GA {x} nai KARA ii
        shushoo{x}.

U1/4:   hatake O motte inai hito WA NE nanka [NE] koojoo TOKA
        [NE]...

U1/4:   ima igiriru DE NE apaato motte iru hito P1/ imasu.

U1/4:   isuramu kyoo NO naka DE NE futatsu guruupu GA aru.

U1/4:   jibun DE NE jibun DE okane ima tsukutte imasu.

U1/4:   kangaekata WA NE.

U1/4:   kuni WA NE dakara komatte iru.

U1/4:   nanka NE...

U1/4:   okane WA toreru kedo demo {cotton} WA NE momen momen.

U1/4:   pakisutan DEWA NE {BMW} TOKA [a] {BMW} [NE]

U1/4:   pakisutan WA NE

U1/4:   tatoeba indo TO kurabete TOKA NE...

U1/4:   TOKA NE

U1/4:	TOKA NE
U1/4:	tokidoki NE [ano] uchi GA kookyoo NO yoo desu.
U1/4:	warui mondai WA NE shite imasen.
U1/4:	watashi GA sunde iru tokai WA NE
U1/4:	yushu shite pakisutan WA NE yushu wata O yushu shite.
U1/4:	zenbu DE NE...
U1/4:	{BMW} NE...
U1/4:	{partly} ajia NO kuniguni WA NE mada dentooteki.